The Archaeology of Collective Action

The American Experience in Archaeological Perspective

D0992615

UNIVERSITY PRESS OF FLORIDA

Florida A&M University, Tallahassee
Florida Atlantic University, Boca Raton
Florida Gulf Coast University, Ft. Myers
Florida International University, Miami
Florida State University, Tallahassee
University of Central Florida, Orlando
University of Florida, Gainesville
University of North Florida, Jacksonville
University of South Florida, Tampa
University of West Florida, Pensacola

The American Experience in Archaeological Perspective

Edited by Michael S. Nassaney

The books in this series explore an event, process, setting, or institution that was significant in the formative experience of contemporary America. Each volume will frame the topic beyond an individual site and attempt to give the reader a flavor of the theoretical, methodological, and substantive issues that researchers face in their examination of that topic or theme. These books will be comprehensive overviews that will allow serious students and scholars to get a good sense of contemporary and past inquiries on a broad theme in American history and culture.

The Archaeology of Collective Action, by Dean J. Saitta (2007)

The Archaeology of Collective Action

Dean J. Saitta

Foreword by Michael S. Nassaney

University Press of Florida
Gainesville/Tallahassee/Tampa/Boca Raton
Pensacola/Orlando/Miami/Jacksonville/Ft. Myers

12 11 10 09 08 07   6 5 4 3 2 1

Library of Congress Cataloging-in-Publication Data
Saitta, Dean J.
The archaeology of collective action / Dean J. Saitta; foreword by
Michael S. Nassaney.
p. cm.—(The American experience in archaeological perspective)
Includes bibliographical references and index.
ISBN 978-0-8130-3070-8 (alk. paper)
    1. Archaeology and history—United States. 2. Social archaeology—
United States. 3. United States—Antiquities. 4. United States—Ethnic
relations. 5. United States—Social conditions. 6. Collective behavior—
History. 7. Coalitions—United States—History. 8. Group identity—
United States—History. 9. National characteristics, American. I. Title.
E159.5.S28 2007
973.0729—dc22   2007001295

The University Press of Florida is the scholarly publishing agency
for the State University System of Florida, comprising Florida A&M
University, Florida Atlantic University, Florida Gulf Coast University,
Florida International University, Florida State University, University
of Central Florida, University of Florida, University of North Florida,
University of South Florida, and University of West Florida.

University Press of Florida
15 Northwest 15th Street
Gainesville, FL 32611-2079
http://www.upf.com

For Martha, Joe, and working families everywhere

Contents

Maps

Figures

Foreword

I often tell my students that archaeology reveals as much about contemporary life as it does about the past. This is a particularly apt observation in regards to the examination of archaeological sites associated with the development of the modern world. It follows that archaeologies of the recent past have a contribution to make to an anthropological understanding of the American experience. The purpose of this series is to highlight the results of that research and make it available to a wider audience.

Considerable work has been conducted on post-Columbian archaeological sites in the United States since the 1960s. Federal legislation and the establishment of the Society for Historical Archaeology have encouraged the investigation of sites associated with all Americans, regardless of social class, race, ethnicity, or gender. The result has been broadened public inclusion and an expanded conception of our national heritage. Historical archaeology is now poised to provide anthropological understandings of our nation's formative cultural and social developments; it is no longer merely a handmaiden of history.

In their efforts to preserve and organize culture's clutter, historical archaeologists have located, identified, analyzed, and interpreted the detritus of countless events, processes, settings, and institutions that were significant in laying the foundations of contemporary America. Because that residue was not edited for content, it can inform on the histories, cultures, and social identities of a broad cast of characters who were actively involved in the making of America. A critical reading of this material record brings into focus processes of conflict and cooperation, power and resistance, struggle and accommodation. These stories are familiar, though not always consonant with the officially sanctioned ones that comprise the dominant narratives many of us were taught.

By examining the American experience from an archaeological perspective, we are afforded the opportunity to read between the lines of the documentary record to shed new light on the forces that shaped the American psyche. Of course, the historical and material outcomes of these influences were by no means monolithic; there have always been alternative and competing visions of American values, beliefs, customs, and relations that created social, political, economic, and ideological tensions. The historical contingencies of the American experience in the past and the present challenge us to imagine new future possibilities.

The backdrop for the American experience since the industrial revolution has been capitalism and the struggle between workers (labor) and managers (capital). Industrialization, harsh working conditions, low wages, and the de-skilling of the labor process galvanized a working-class consciousness that often led to collective action, which challenged the political and economic forces that attempted to create and maintain structural inequalities. Concessions such as the right to collective bargaining and safer working conditions were gained from these struggles. History shows that these rights were neither inevitable nor won without a fight. Nowhere is this more apparent than in the coalfields of southern Colorado.

In *The Archaeology of Collective Action,* Dean Saitta employs an explanatory and emancipatory archaeology to carefully craft an exposé of an important, violent, and partially forgotten chapter in American history—the Colorado coalfield strike and war of 1913–14, including the Ludlow Massacre. Recent investigations by Saitta and his coworkers (sometimes referred to as the Ludlow Collective) have focused on the remains of a tent colony that was fired upon by the state militia in 1914, as well as investigations of related sites. Cognizant of the need to tack between the past and the present, the individual and the collective, the scientific and the humanistic, Saitta explicates how a materialist and pragmatist epistemology can be used to illuminate capitalist social relations while simultaneously connecting archaeology to contemporary life and diversifying its public audience. Archaeological evidence at multiple scales speaks to the everyday lives and relationships of an ethnically diverse group of coal miners and their families and to the collective strategies of resistance they employed to further their cause against capital.

This story and the analytical approach that Saitta uses to unravel it are important for several reasons. First, the study foregrounds the contributions that historically marginalized groups have made to the American experience—a hallmark of American historical archaeology. Second, the project benefits from the support and cooperation of the United Mine Workers of America and the descendant communities of coal miners and other working families in the region. The project is clearly more than just an academic exercise; it has a strong public, emancipatory component. In Saitta's own words, it promotes "reflection upon the present in ways that can help realize human freedom, potential, and dignity." Third, and perhaps most important for this series, the study makes the results of historical archaeological research accessible to a wide audience. In doing so, it demonstrates how historical archaeology can play a role in reclaiming and expanding the space for labor history in public memory while contributing to a richer appreciation and more nuanced understanding of the American mosaic.

Michael S. Nassaney
Series Editor

Preface and Acknowledgments

A central driving interest of modern archaeology is the role played by in-dividual actors—human agents—in processes of social change. A focus on individuals and their coping strategies in particular historical contexts has expanded and enriched archaeological interpretation. It has moved the disci-pline away from normative, bloodless models of "cultural systems" and other abstractions toward more nuanced and human-scale models. Like all other theoretical frameworks, however, agency theory has its limitations and blind spots. One of these blind spots is the role of *collective* action—the group be-havior of individuals united by particular life experiences, existential anxieties, and strategic interests—in shaping social life and change.

This book examines historical archaeology's success in reconstructing col-lective social action and considers the implications of these reconstructions for society today. The touchstone for considering such collective behavior is historical archaeology's great triumvirate of social identities: race, gender, and class. Much progress has been made by historical archaeologists in illumi-nating race-, gender-, and class-based forms of collective action in the past. These struggles have been central to the American experience. They have pro-foundly shaped our sense of others, ourselves, and America's place in world history. This book selectively reviews some of this progress, and then adds to our understanding of class-based collective action by presenting an original archaeological case study of the Colorado coalfield strike and war of 1913–14. In so doing, it underscores the relevance of archaeologies of collective action in current disciplinary and larger societal contexts. The book is aimed at that rapidly expanding audience of scholars, students, and citizens who see archae-ology as both a source of historical truth and a comment on the contemporary human condition.

Although written by a single author, this book is the result of a collective undertaking. It incorporates many ideas and insights that have been percolat-ing over the past ten years among colleagues and students associated with the Colorado Coalfield War Archaeological Project. This first-of-a-kind archaeo-logical study of sites associated with the Colorado coalfield strike is a collabo-ration between faculty and students at the University of Denver, Binghamton University, and Fort Lewis College. The Coalfield War Project is a work in progress. Original fieldwork was conducted between 1997 and 2002, but laboratory analysis of collected artifacts and dissemination of research results is ongoing.

My colleagues Philip Duke (Fort Lewis College) and Randy McGuire (Binghamton University) were instrumental in getting the Coalfield War Project off the ground. The original idea for the project was Randy's. Among other benefits, it allowed him to join his friends for collaborative work in the state where he was raised. Phil hosted our spirited planning sessions and has been a steady source of insight and wise counsel. For all three of us, the project is a labor of love that offers relief from the rest of our day jobs as professors and prehistorians. It provides a unique opportunity for us to bring together our passions for dirt archaeology, critical social theory, and service to the public good.

The Coalfield War Project has been blessed with two superb project directors. Mark Walker planned and oversaw the initial archaeological fieldwork. He has also been our best thinker about the place of coalfield war events in national public memory. Karin Burd Larkin succeeded Mark and coordinated an enormous amount of laboratory analysis, public interpretative text preparation, and report writing. Mark's and Karin's hands are especially prominent in chapters 6 and 7. Like Mark, Paul Reckner and Margaret Wood were present at the creation. Their dissertation work substantively advanced the Coalfield War Project. Bonnie Clark directed fieldwork in 2001 while a graduate student at the University of California, Berkeley. Today, as my faculty colleague at the University of Denver, she advises students working with project material. The work of Bonnie's student Amie Gray on Ludlow ceramics is prominently featured in chapter 6. Mike Jacobson's dissertation work at Binghamton University on the spatial organization of the Ludlow colony also informs and enriches that chapter. Other students who have contributed to the body of coalfield war scholarship are Sarah Chicone, Claire Horn, Summer Moore, and Beth Rudden. Expert field supervision was provided by field assistants Donna Bryant, Kristen Jones, and Jason Lapham.

We are grateful to several individuals for specialized field and lab analyses. My faculty colleague Larry Conyers conducted ground-penetrating radar work at Ludlow, as did his student Craig Stoner. Mona Charles of Fort Lewis College conducted site magnetometer work. April Beisaw and Andrea Kozub of Binghamton University conducted faunal analyses, and Erin Saar of the University of Denver performed ammunition analysis.

The Colorado Coalfield War Archaeological Project has been generously supported with eight years of grants from the Colorado Historical Society–State Historical Fund. Thomas Carr was an expert, compassionate technical specialist. Binghamton University supported the archaeological fieldwork with a faculty development grant, as did the University of Denver's Faculty Research Fund. The Walter Rosenberry Fund and the Humanities Institute of the Division of Arts, Humanities, and Social Sciences at the University of Denver generously supported site interpretation and public education projects. A number of community institutions supported the work, including the Colorado Endowment for the Humanities, the Colorado Digitization Project, and the Trinidad History Museum. The archaeological work at Berwind was conducted with the permission of Southern Colorado Realty. Trinidad State Junior College provided, at special rates, room and board for fieldworkers.

This book is informed by discussions among participants in two Colorado Endowment for the Humanities Summer Teacher Institutes on American labor history. For their ideas and insights, thanks are owed participating scholars Joe Bonacquista, Silvio Caputo, Joanne Dodds, Sybil Downing, Philip Duke, Jay Fell, Julie Greene, Randall McGuire, Laurel Vartebedian, Mark Walker, Margaret Wood, and Zeese Papanikolas. I thank CEH director Maggie Coval, her staff, and my former colleagues on the CEH Board of Directors for their belief in, and support of, our work.

I am indebted to several mentors who guided me in the intellectual odyssey that has resulted in this book. They have been a constant source of inspiration and advice. To Barbara Bender, Art Keene, Mark Leone, Tom Patterson, Bob Paynter, and Martin Wobst: my heartfelt thanks.

The Coalfield War Project could not have happened without the cooperation of the United Mine Workers of America. Excavation at the Ludlow Massacre Memorial was conducted with the permission of UMWA District 22, UMWA Local 9856, and Local 9856's women's auxiliary. Carol Blatnick-Barros, Mike Romero, and Yolanda Romero were generous local contacts in Trinidad, Colorado. Bob Butero offered friendship and support in the UMWA's Denver office. Cecil Roberts presides over the UMWA from Washington, D.C., but he is always with us in spirit and never failed to inspire with his appearances at the annual Ludlow Memorial Service.

The descendant communities of coal miners and other working families in southern Colorado have been a steady source of support. Their oral histories and other bits of local knowledge helped guide the field archaeology at the Berwind coal camp and the Ludlow tent colony. Their input continues to enrich site interpretation. Many other educators, editorialists, writers, poets, filmmakers, newspaper reporters, and citizens in Colorado and beyond have sustained us with their interest and encouragement. There is something in the story of the coalfield war that resonates with many people. The requests for public talks and presentations have, at times, been almost overwhelming. Certainly, the recent tragedies at the Sago and Alma coal mines in West Virginia and at the Darby mine in Harlan County, Kentucky, indicate that the coal mining past is, in many ways, still present.

My own family has been infinitely patient with losing Dad to summer days in the coalfield, weekday evenings on the local lecture circuit, and weekends at the computer. I am deeply appreciative of the support of my wife, Martha Rooney Saitta, and our young son, Joe.

1

Archaeology as an Explanatory and Emancipatory Enterprise

Twenty years ago, in an article entitled "The Ancient Maya and the Political Present," Richard Wilk argued that archaeology has a dual nature (Wilk 1985). On the one hand, it is a search for objective, verifiable knowledge about the past. Archaeologists use explicitly formulated theory and method to clarify and expand our understanding of human history. There can be a lot of latitude for doing so, given today's generally accepted philosophical axiom that all knowledge of the past requires a "rich theoretical judgment" about the meaning of available evidence (Wylie 1989: 100). Indeed, sometimes very different theories can be equally effective in explaining archaeological data. But even allowing that all knowledge is underdetermined by available data, a general consensus exists that there is a real world that constrains what we can say about it. There are facts of the matter to be appropriated, and it is the goal of scientific archaeology to parlay the facts within its domain into historical truth.

On the other hand, archaeology for Wilk is also an irreducibly human enterprise. It is embedded in culture. It is performed by people who bring conscious and unconscious hopes, desires, and biases to the table. Archaeology is socially constituted in complex ways, which influences the theoretical judgments used to give meaning to archaeological data. As Wilk frames it, archaeology conducts an "informal and often hidden political and philosophical dialogue" with the major issues of contemporary life (1985: 308). Indeed, archaeology has even been shown to conduct this dialogue from a particular social position. Several comprehensive historical analyses reveal that archaeology has always been a middle-class enterprise, produced by and for that social class (Trigger 1989; Patterson 1995; see also Gosden 2004). Studies of popular magazines such as *Archaeology* and *National Geographic* indicate readerships that are 60 percent college degreed, with 80 percent employed as professional administrators and managers (McGuire and Walker 1999: 163). Because of archaeology's status as a middle-class profession, archaeological accounts of the past often reflect middle-class anxieties and concerns over population size, climate change, energy shortages, and so on.

Archaeology's embeddedness in society, and its particular middle-class position, means that it has serious political currency. Wilk (1985: 319) reminds us of George Orwell's epigram from *Nineteen Eighty Four*: "Who controls the past controls the future; who controls the present controls the past." Knowledge of pasts that, because of data scarcity, require particularly rich theoretical judgments about "the way things were"—such as the time period of earliest human evolution—are especially amenable to justifying ideas about the "natural" form of gender roles, family organization, economic life, political structure, intergroup social relations, and so on. Knowledge of the past can be and has been used in different ways by various interest groups looking to pursue particular social agendas. It has been used to legitimate, oppress, and liberate (Gathercole and Lowenthal 1990; Kohl and Fawcett 1995).

Today's globalizing world has further complicated matters for archaeologists (Gosden 2004). Globalization has produced an expansion of archaeology's audience beyond the middle class in ways not entirely comfortable for those working in the discipline's mainstream. Many historically marginalized groups—such as indigenous peoples subjugated by colonialist empires, or the descendants of African slaves and working-class immigrants—are taking an interest in archaeology. Aware of archaeology's class position and historical ties to colonialist projects, descendant communities are putting pressure on archaeologists to write pasts that acknowledge the history, humanity, and creativity of the ancestors and to incorporate traditional knowledge and voices into those narratives. In North America, the Native American Graves Protection and Repatriation Act (NAGPRA) has challenged Western scientific ways of knowing more directly and intensely than ever before. Archaeologists are not only being required to return sacred objects and other cultural patrimony to Indian tribes but also being called upon to better justify what they do and the criteria they use for favoring some understandings of the past over others.

Thus, archaeological work is neither philosophically innocent nor socially inconsequential. It has impacts upon and implications for the present and must respond to a growing number of external constituencies. The question is not *whether* archaeology is political, but *how* it is so. The notion that archaeology is a socially embedded and mediated practice was controversial at one time but today is widely accepted, thanks to those who have established that all knowledge is constructed and contextual (for example, Gero, Lacy, and Blakey 1983; Saitta 1983; Shanks and Tilley 1987a, 1987b; contributors to Pinsky and Wylie 1989). There is nothing in this analysis of archaeology's nature—and Wilk is careful to point this out—that threatens the scientific rationality of the field. Recognizing the social context of archaeology helps us to better explain where interpretive theories come from and forces us to systematically explore the biases that influence our own interpretations. The challenge for archaeologists is to be aware of their discipline's dual nature, take responsibility for it, and be vigilant about how archaeological knowledge is used by others.

This situation is producing not only greater self-consciousness about what we do but also explicitly activist approaches that recognize archaeology's potential as a force for positive social change. Wilk touches on this potential in discussing the ways in which the past can be used as a *charter*, that is, a set of guides for how contemporary society might organize itself differently to cope with various existential problems (Wilk 1985: 319). The definition of the term *positive*, of course, depends on the intellectual and social position of the knower. For some, archaeology can help confront "the practices and ideological structures that promote inequality in the world at large" (Paynter 2000a: 4) by challenging the historical reconstructions that support such practices and structures (Little 1997; Matthews, Leone, and Jordan 2002). This is the view adopted in this book. There is nothing in such manifestos for a *critical archaeology* (Leone 1986; Leone, Potter, and Shackel 1987; Palus, Leone, and Cochran 2006) to suggest that political activism requires an abandonment of archaeology's responsibility to produce scientific truth. The constraints imposed by real-world data, our awareness that archaeology can serve and has served political agendas, and the fact that scientific communities rarely if ever suffer from a shortage of skeptics pretty much guarantees that the rationality of the field will be preserved.

All things considered, I think of critical archaeology as being an *explanatory* and *emancipatory* enterprise: explanatory, in the sense of producing causal knowledge of the past that respects accumulated data; emancipatory, in the sense of promoting reflection upon the present in ways that can help realize human freedom, potential, and dignity (Wright 1993). A critical archaeology illuminates the variable social consequences of the political, economic, and cultural relationships that have organized human life in particular times and places and clarifies how the present came to be (Palus, Leone, and Cochran 2006). It works to expose the otherness or alterity of the past so as to foster different thinking about the future (see also Hodder 1999: 208–9). It sees the discovery of otherness as best accomplished by welcoming new parties—such as the historically marginalized groups mentioned above—into the conversation (Walker 2003; Gosden 2004; Palus, Leone, and Cochran 2006). So informed, and when coupled with strong public outreach initiatives, a critically engaged archaeology stands to improve science and impel positive social change. Critical archaeology is an archaeology of hearts and minds; it is a moral as well as scientific enterprise.

Historical archaeology is especially well positioned to extend this emancipatory project. Historical archaeology, more than any other branch of the discipline, is concerned with the production of knowledge about ourselves: our social and historical contexts and the material shape and direction of our world (Delle, Mrozowski, and Paynter 2000a). It studies the social relations and contradictions that have produced contemporary inequalities in the distribution of material resources and human life chances (Nassaney and Abel 2000; Palus, Leone, and Cochran 2006). It also engages, more widely than other fields, the living descendants of subject populations (Orser 2001; Wilkie 2005). In the past decade, many historical archaeologists have advocated, and demonstrated the virtues of, working directly with groups having an intimate local connection to the sites we study (Potter 1992; Spector 1993; LaRoche and Blakey 1997; McDavid 1997; contributors to Hall and Silliman 2006a).

To extend this project, some historical archaeologists have explicitly confronted the global socioeconomic system that affects, in some way, life for everyone on the planet today: capitalism. Capitalism is responsible for the differential distributions of wealth and poverty observable in the recent archaeological record. A focus on capitalism foregrounds social divisions and conflicts and their embodiment in material culture. Several recent studies have established capitalism as an appropriate analytical focus for historical archaeology (Paynter 1988; Little 1994; Leone 1995; Orser 1996; contributors to Leone and Potter 1999; Delle, Mrozowski, and Paynter 2000a; Matthews, Leone, and Jordan 2002). Others have marshaled the philosophical and empirical warrants for developing a critical historical archaeology of capitalism. Contributors to Leone and Potter 1999, for example, take an explicitly activist approach to their subject matter. They are concerned that their scholarship illuminates capitalism in ways that can demystify its operation, if not actually help to transform it. They do this by paying attention to local variation in the way people cope with capitalism's differentiating processes, while being mindful of global-scale relationships that shape the local. A critical historical archaeology is one that brings the lived experience of women, people of color, and workers into view, in a way that debunks the myth that we are all middle class (Paynter 2000b). Its practitioners have produced new insights about the recent past and encouraged greater self-consciousness about the social value and political utility of archaeology (chapter 4).

This orientation offers new possibilities for connecting archaeology to contemporary life and for diversifying archaeology's public audience. Such critical projects require us to reflect upon our own "taken-for-granteds" as concerns ways of living and thinking (Paynter 2000a). Perhaps most importantly, they give these taken-for-granteds a history. As Brumfiel (2003: 214) puts it, critical archaeologies destabilize explanations of how things came to be—especially those that are hardening into self-serving dogma—by focusing on times and places when social arrangements were "still in flux, thus revealing their artificial and arbitrary nature." In other words, they reveal the contingent nature of social life and change, and how things could have turned out very differently. In so doing, such accounts show us that we are not stuck with what we have. They remind us that there are always multiple ways of organizing social life and that current relationships can be undone (Matthews, Leone, and Jordan 2002). In short, they strengthen our license to participate in history.

This book extends this critical and activist project by exploring the nature of collective action as reconstructed by historical archaeology. *Collective action* is defined as the group behavior of individuals united by particular life experiences, existential anxieties, and strategic interests in concrete historical (political, economic, and cultural) circumstances. My primary interest is in collective action that emanates "from below": the kind that challenges the political and economic forces that marginalize, disenfranchise, and oppress. Of course, we can also do an archaeology of collective action "from above": one that focuses on the power of elites and the strategies they use to oppress and exploit. Pollack and Bernbeck (forthcoming) have recently called for such an "archaeology of perpetrators," on the belief that understanding how dominant groups "tick" is just as important as understanding what motivates resistors if the goal is to remedy social injustice. Some of the insights produced by an archaeology of perpetrators will be drawn upon throughout this book.

The touchstones for considering collective action by resistors as well as perpetrators is historical anthropology's great triumvirate of gender, race, and class (Scott 1994; Delle, Mrozowski, and Paynter 2000a; Paynter 2000b). These axes of social identity are the primary ones along which material resources and life chances are differentially distributed in the modern world. My governing questions include the following. How have archaeologists analyzed collective action vis-à-vis gender-, race-, and class-based power differentials in the past? How have dominated or marginalized groups coped with these differentials via collective action and its related material interferences, that is, the *artifacts* that people use to "change something from what it was to what they thought it should be . . . or that would change in undesirable directions if artifacts did not interfere" (Wobst 2000: 42; see also chapter 3)? What do we learn from various kinds of collective action in the past that might serve change agendas today? What contemporary social identities and alliances are most in need of nurturing, and how can we best cultivate them? These questions spring

naturally from a critical archaeology of collective action and promise to expand the discipline's relevance for contemporary society. I examine historical
archaeology's success in reconstructing collective social action in the past and
consider the implications of these reconstructions for intervening in contemporary social life.

The book is organized as follows. Chapter 2 details the philosophical orientation that supports a critical, emancipatory archaeology. This orientation
is broadly pragmatist. I take for granted that there is a real past about which
we can produce secure knowledge. But, as noted above, knowledge is both
constructed (dependent upon theoretical extensions beyond observables) and
contextual (shaped by contemporary social conditions and trends). Pragmatists pay attention to the consequences of theory for living as well as knowing.
Accordingly, the social causes and consequences of archaeological knowledge
are as legitimate a target of critique as the theories and methods that give
meaning to archaeological data. Pragmatists are also concerned with knowledge proffered by groups historically marginalized by the scientific community. While "their" knowledge is just as constructed and contextual as "our"
knowledge and contains its own unique tensions and pitfalls, comparative
study of the particulars offers promise for drawing out the otherness of the
past.

Chapter 3 covers some basic theoretical and methodological issues in the
archaeological study of collective action. It puts scholarly concern for collective action into historical context and explains why collective action is an
important and compelling research topic at the present time. It details a particular theory of material culture that is helpful for tracking collective action
in the archaeological record and sets forth the methodological commitments
by which theories of society and material culture are connected to archaeological data so as to give meaning to the past.

Chapter 4 reviews some substantive contributions that historical archaeologists have made to our understanding of race-, gender-, and class-based
collective action in the American past. These studies focus on a variety of
social contexts, including southern plantations, urban neighborhoods, and
industrial workshops. The examples are selective, chosen with an eye for those
that connect especially well to the detailed archaeological case study offered in
chapter 6.

Chapter 5 sets the stage for that case study by providing background history on the Colorado coalfield strike of 1913–14. The Colorado strike—which
climaxed in the death of women and children at the Ludlow striker's colony
on April 20, 1914, an event known as the Ludlow Massacre—stands as perhaps
the most dramatic example of open class warfare in American history. The

strike involved some of the most charismatic and powerful personalities in American history, including the industrialist John D. Rockefeller Jr., the labor activist Mary "Mother" Jones, and the novelist and social critic Upton Sinclair. Although the strike ended in defeat for the striking miners, the episode was a turning point in labor-management relations throughout the United States. Yet for all their significance in shaping the American experience, the events in southern Colorado are relatively unknown outside the circle of professional historians. The Colorado coalfield troubles are surely part of the hidden or submerged history of the American West (Walker 2000, 2003).

Chapter 6 discusses how archaeology at coalfield war sites is contributing to our understanding of labor struggle on America's industrializing frontier and, more generally, of class-based collective action. It summarizes selected analyses of excavated material and how these analyses supplement and correct both official and folk histories of coalfield events.

Chapter 7 moves from the past to the present, from the explanatory to the emancipatory. It picks up Wilk's "dialogue with the present" theme by considering how coalfield war research articulates with contemporary struggles for workplace rights in southern Colorado and beyond. The Coalfield War Project is itself an exercise in collaborative teaching and research, as well as community engagement. It brings project participants into close contact with the descendent community of coal miners in southeastern Colorado, especially United Mine Workers of America Local 9865. The chapter describes the historical circumstances that occasioned this involvement and how archaeology is shaping public memory of the 1914 strike in ways that serve the cause of better history and better critical thinking about the present.

The concluding chapter considers why the study of collective action matters for a discipline whose demonstrable and widely perceived status as a middle-class, leisure-time activity continually threatens it with irrelevance and for a society always poised—as a result of rampant individualism and group identity politics—on the edge of atomism and fragmentation. It offers some thoughts on how we might develop research on collective action to benefit society and increase archaeology's stock as a socially relevant enterprise.

2

Philosophical Commitments
of a Critical Archaeology

This chapter details the philosophical orientation that supports a critical, emancipatory archaeology. The widening acknowledgment over the past twenty years of archaeology's dual nature has been accompanied by a sea change in philosophy and theory. Several important critiques (Shanks and Tilley 1987a, 1987b; contributors to Pinsky and Wylie 1989; Preucel 1991) have moved archaeology away from empiricist and positivist epistemologies to various realist alternatives. These alternatives (1) appreciate knowledge as constructed and as produced from particular social standpoints; (2) support, because of standpoint sensitivity, theoretical inquiries into gender, race, class, and other structuring relationships in human life; (3) recognize that, even though empirical data constrain what we can say about the past, there can still be lots of room for interpretation; and (4) demand, because of theory's underdetermination by data, broader criteria of evaluation beyond an interpretation's correspondence with archaeological facts and its logical coherence. The influence of the recent postmodern turn in intellectual life is evident here, but so are influences emanating from many other post-positivist philosophies of science.

These philosophical commitments have recently come together in what is being promoted as a *social archaeology* (contributors to Meskell and Preucel 2004a; see also Nassaney 2002). Social archaeology adds a more thorough-going interest in how different people inscribe meaning in space and time and, through these processes of inscription, construct themselves (Meskell and Preucel 2004b: 16). It looks to engage multiple interests in the past, especially those of historically disenfranchised groups. These include all those indigenous and descendant populations marginalized and muted (Little 1997) by expanding capitalism: groups that have been described as "people without history" (Wolf 1982) and "those of little note" (Scott 1994). Social archaeology is thus a more inclusive, democratic practice that appreciates "the multiple entailments of our being-in-the-world" (Meskell and Preucel 2004a: 3). Walker (2003) and Gosden (2004) articulate why this is not only good politics but also good science. Our ability to grasp and learn from the otherness of the past can be enhanced by an engagement with traditional knowledges. In Bernstein's (1988: 388) words, "it is only by the serious encounter with what is other, different, and alien that we can hope to determine what is idiosyncratic, limited, and partial." While engagement with those "outside the guild" (Walker 2003: 76) offers its own frustrations and challenges, it nonetheless makes us aware of silences in the past that we have been creating and opens up new research directions. Such engagement is right at home in a critical archaeology that is both explanatory and emancipatory.

Pragmatist Philosophy: Archaeology and the Problems of Men

I find pragmatist philosophical principles to be especially compatible with, and indeed crucial for advancing, a critical social archaeology. There are many debates about what the fathers of pragmatism (Charles Pierce, William James, John Dewey) meant and about the accuracy of various contemporary interpretations (for example, those of Richard Bernstein and, especially, Richard Rorty). For me, John Dewey captures the essence of the approach with his notion that pragmatism turns from the "problems of philosophy" to the "problems of men" (Dewey 1917: 230). That is, it applies itself less toward knowing or "getting things right" (in terms of capturing some final transcendental truth) than toward living or "making things new" (Rorty 1989: 78). For pragmatists, making things new requires that we improve our ability to respond to the views, interests, and concerns of ever larger groups of diverse human beings— to expand the scope of who counts as "one of us" (Rorty 1991: 38).

Thus, I take pragmatism as seamlessly dovetailing with the kind of sensibility that equips us for using the craft of archaeology (*sensu* Shanks and McGuire 1996: 82–83: a "unified practice of hand, heart, mind" and "emotion, need, desire") to address human needs. Pragmatism does so without abandoning time-honored and still useful concepts of truth, experience, and testing. Instead, it reformulates these concepts in a way that is more sensitive to meeting human need. In so doing, it responds more directly—and perhaps more coherently and honestly—to the widespread consensus that archaeological work occurs in a political context and that we must therefore be aware of how the results of our inquiries are used within that context. A brief summary of core pragmatist philosophical commitments follows.

The first commitment is to an antifoundational notion of truth—the idea that there are no fixed, stable grounds on which knowledge-claims can be established. Truth is not an accurate reflection of something nonhuman (Rorty 1989, 1991); rather, it is a matter of intersubjective consensus among human beings, one mediated by currently available theories, methods, and data. This notion produces a warrant for aggressively experimenting with theory and method to arrive at historical truth. Experimentation is crucial for improving and expanding the conversation between and among interested parties of scientists and citizens. The vitality of this conversation is what moves archaeology and its constituencies toward the sorts of "usable truths" that can serve human need. So understood, pragmatism moves us in directions other than those stipulated by the earliest commentators on archaeology's social relevance. Ford (1973: 93), for example, saw the "indiscriminant publication of unverified hunches" in the discipline as an obstacle to archaeology's ability to serve humanity. Alternatively, I think that liberal production and publication of such hunches—the more the merrier—is critical for advancing archaeology's explanatory and emancipatory project.

The second core commitment is to the idea that truth-claims must be evaluated against a broader notion of experience. Specifically, they must be evaluated in terms of their concrete consequences for life today—for how we want to live as a pluralistic community. Instead of simply asking whether a claim about the past is empirically sufficient in light of available data, pragmatism asks what difference the claim makes to how we want to live. What are the implications of theoretical claims from evolutionary archaeology, interpretive archaeology, or indeed, any other current framework for understanding society and history for how we think about, and how we might intervene in, human social life? To what extent does a truth-claim expeditiously meet the human needs at stake in, say, reburial or repatriation controversies; that is, to what extent does it facilitate putting human souls to rest and human minds at ease? Experience, in this view, is relational, interactive, and creative. It acknowledges our status as social and historical beings; it is genuinely reflexive (Kloppenberg 1996). Defining experience in this way means that we must subsume the usual realist criterial rationality for judging truth-claims (that is, criteria emphasizing logical coherence and correspondence between theory and data) under something that is still broadly criterial but much more qualitative and humanistic—what some have called "fuzzy" rationality (see Rorty 1991: 38).

A third commitment is to a particular notion of *testing*, specifically as it relates to the evaluation of truth-claims produced by different standpoints, perspectives, and cultural traditions. As noted, especially germane to archaeology these days are those truth-claims that divide scientific and various descendant community knowledges of the past, including indigenous, immigrant, working-class, and other folk knowledges. Zimmerman (2001) argues that within archaeology there is no clear epistemology for "coalescing" descendant community and mainstream scientific understandings of the past. Others have also advocated a rethinking of epistemology now that previously disenfranchised groups have places at the table (for example, Schuldenrein 1999). In contrast to the mainstream scientific view in which competing ideas are tested against each other in light of the empirical record, pragmatism stipulates that we test the ideas of other cultures and descendant communities by weaving them together with ones we already have (Rorty 1991). Testing is a matter of inter-weaving and continually reweaving webs of belief to increasingly expand and deepen community and, perhaps, create new fields of possible action (Rouse 2003: 101). Pragmatism prescribes a "measured relativism" (Appleby, Hunt, and Jacob 1994: 284) that balances a commitment to evaluation with the parallel belief that cultural pluralism is our best recipe for civil cohesion (Menand 1997: xxviii). Latour (1999: 4) captures what I think is the same basic idea with his notion of a "sturdy relativism" in which science allows us to be sure of many things but also seeks to make better connections with the wider social collective. For Latour, this relativism is not one that capitulates to "anything goes" or, in his words, to the "frantic disorderly mob" (1999: 22).

The specter of objectivity haunts these core philosophical commitments. What does objectivity mean in this context? And do we abandon all hope of attaining it by embracing a pragmatist orientation? The notion of objectivity endorsed by pragmatists, as alluded to above, is one that Megill (1994) describes as dialectical. Dialectical objectivity takes a particular stance toward the subjectivity of the knower. Whereas other kinds of objectivity seek to either exclude subjectivity (absolute objectivity) or contain it (disciplinary objectivity), dialectical objectivity adopts a positive attitude toward subjectivity. Subjectivity is seen as indispensable to the constituting of objects, as in fact necessary for objectivity. As Heidegger (1927) noted, objects first become known to us through action in the world. Knowing is thus acting, and human acting is always acting in company (Fabian 1994). These arguments close the loop to a concept of "objective truth" as a matter of intersubjective consensus—or solidarity—among human beings, rather than as a matter of accurate reflection of something nonhuman.

This pragmatist notion of objectivity differs a bit from realist notions that are widely invoked in contemporary archaeology. Realist objectivity stipulates that there is an independent reality, that alternative accounts map it differently, and that although hope and bias complicate the picture, systematic exploration of similarity and difference can establish credible knowledge-claims and produce more complete understandings of the past. Binford (1982a; see also 1982b) characterized this kind of objectivity as "operational objectivity." This qualified notion of objectivity is today endorsed by archaeologists across the paradigmatic spectrum. Thus, processualists embrace "mitigated objectivity" (Clark 1998: 22), contextualists "guarded objectivity" (Hodder 1991c: 10) or "modified objectivity" (Hodder and Hutson 2003: 223), and feminists "embodied objectivity" (Wylie 1995: 271).

The rub is that such notions of objectivity, no matter how well qualified, still might not be best for regulating a more democratic, inclusive, and critical social archaeology. Pragmatism's commitment to testing the beliefs of other cultures by interweaving and continually reweaving them with beliefs that we already have best dovetails with the indigenous archaeologist's sensible suggestion (Watkins 1998: 23), offered in response to the scientific archaeologist (Clark 1998), that we settle differences between indigenous and scientific knowledges by finding a "path between trees," rather than by bulldozing the forest or circumventing it altogether. The navigational guide in these encounters is something fully human—wider, deeper, stronger, and better community—rather than some socially independent object that we seek to accurately represent in theory.

Practicing Pragmatics

How can a pragmatist archaeology concretely serve this enlargement of community, especially when many public constituencies are utterly indifferent to whether archaeology exists—or not? How can we navigate a path between trees in the new, postcolonial world identified by Gosden (2004)?

One obvious way is through the production of knowledge that takes stock of neglected peoples and histories and that focuses on questions other than the kinds of "origins questions"—about the evolution of humanity, agriculture, and civilization—that have traditionally anchored archaeology's more popular writing (see also Meskell and Preucel 2004c: 324). Of interest are questions about the "lived experience" of everyday life—its conditions, variations, rhythms, and disjunctions—with answers developed in such a way that they are accessible to those living peoples having a stake in the interpretations. As Wylie (1995) points out, this ambition is only realizable if those whose lives are affected are directly involved in the research enterprise as partners and collaborators, instead of just subjects or informants. Archaeology has been making good progress in reaching out to these groups. New understandings of the past are being developed by the subaltern archaeologies of women and racialized "others" (chapter 4), and by anticolonialist archaeologies focused on indigenous peoples and their histories (Schmidt and Patterson 1995).

The efforts of myself and my colleagues, detailed in chapters 6 and 7 of this book, to develop a working-class archaeology are cut from similar cloth (see also Duke and Saitta 1998; McGuire and Walker 1999; Ludlow Collective 2001). Our critical history of early-twentieth-century coal miners in southern Colorado is one that we offer as an antidote to official histories of the West. Official histories—especially in the American West—are nationalist, progressive, and triumphal, emphasizing social unity and continuity of the existing social order and its institutions (Bodnar 1992). They gloss over periods of transformation and rupture or spin those ruptures (for example, the Civil War) as always having produced a better society, "a more perfect union." In contrast, critical histories deal with context, transformation, and rupture, addressing both the historical process and different narratives about that process (Trouillot 1995). Both kinds of history often conflict with *vernacular* (Bodnar 1992) histories of the past. Vernacular histories are local histories derived from the firsthand, everyday experience of those people who were directly involved with history's events. They are "passed around the kitchen table," conveying "what social reality feels like rather than what it should be like" (Bodnar 1992: 14). Vernacular histories threaten the sacred and timeless nature of official history, just as critical history threatens vernacular history (chapter 7).

Our archaeological work in the Colorado coalfield brings us into dialogue with people—including trade unionists, our primary clients—steeped in vernacular history. The vast majority of them have never had much use for archaeology, realist or otherwise. As one rank-and-filer bluntly put it to me at a 1997 union hall meeting where I went seeking permission to excavate at coalfield sites—and I paraphrase for polite company—"I can tell you everything you need to know about Ludlow in three words—they got [screwed]." The alienation and even hostility apparent in this statement was a wake-up call concerning the realities of working-class life and thought, and it threw into question the wider social value of a pursuit like archaeology. Others in the same unionist company, however, are keenly aware that history is complicated and can be written in many ways, all of them deeply political. "You're not Republicans, are you?" is how one union official framed the concern when Randy McGuire and I first inquired about the possibility of working at Ludlow. Thus, the gulf between academic and working-class cultures in our research area is palpable. We may or may not need a "working-class archaeology," but we seem to need a different way of justifying it. In our case, a key to narrowing the cultural gulf has been to appreciate that Ludlow and other coalfield sites are part of a living history and long commemorative tradition and that they are considered sacred ground by the descendants of miners who lived and died there (chapter 7).

Progress is also being made in coping with the other, arguably more difficult, conflicts in archaeological interpretation, such as those that surround

NAGPRA compliance. These conflicts especially beg for pragmatic interventions more attuned to "living" than "knowing." By law NAGPRA compliance is governed by a realist, criterial rationality. The success of a claim for cultural affiliation depends on whether it is supported by most of the available biological, linguistic, archaeological, and documentary evidence. Happily, in this scheme, native oral traditions are assigned an evidentiary status equal to the other kinds of evidence (see Anyon et al. 1997; Echo-Hawk 2000). However, NAGPRA's "preponderance of evidence" criterion remains deeply problematic, both because of the elastic nature of evidence in archaeology (resulting from the particular quality of archaeological data combined with the fact that such data become evidence only in light of theory) and because of the often deep contentiousness of tribal oral traditions.

Given this situation, a realist, criterial rationality may not be the most appropriate or productive. Instead, we might follow the lead of those pragmatist philosophers and Native Americans who suggest that a more important and relevant criterion is the consequences of knowledge-claims for everyday life: for how we want to live and for the building of a genuinely pluralist community characterized by mutual understanding and respect. At some NAGPRA consultations in Durango, Colorado, in 1998, several Pueblo tribal representatives implicitly endorsed pragmatist evaluative criteria when they argued that history is less important than survival and the maintenance of harmonious relationships among the tribes (Duke 1999). Survival is understood broadly as political, economic, and cultural. Naranjo (1995: 249) takes a similar stand by asserting that, in her view, the Pueblo Indian's primary concern is with "the larger issues of breathing and dying" rather than with the specific details of knowing that focus scientific worldviews. This concern for the present as well as the past—for living as well as knowing—represents a significant convergence between pragmatist and tribal epistemologies that is worth exploiting for its unifying potential. But this unity can be established only if we are willing to rethink the usual scientific criteria—that is, empirical and logical sufficiency—for judging and integrating knowledge-claims.

Other convergences are apparent in the realm of methodology. Speaking at a conference dedicated to the topic of indigenous people and archaeology, Lomaomvaya and Ferguson (2003) note, "In Hopi culture, what stands the test of time is substantive information about the past. Collection and analysis of data requires theory, but for Hopi it is the Hopi past itself that is most important, not what we think this past means for the world beyond Hopi." This primary interest in archaeological "thick description" (Geertz 1973: 6) of a particular past converges with the pragmatist belief that human solidarity is best achieved not by those disciplines—theology, science, philosophy—charged with "penetrating behind the many private appearances to the one general common reality" but by those that sensitize humans to the experience of diverse "others" through exploration of the private and idiosyncratic (Rorty 1989: 94). Rorty (1989: 94) notes that "novels and ethnographies" are especially well suited to building this kind of solidarity. It seems to me that archaeological narratives attuned to human cultural variability across space and time, and developed via the particular reflexive and hermeneutic methodology described in the next chapter, can be just as useful.

Despite its critique of criterial rationality and preference for thick description over nomothetics, the pragmatist alternative need not be antiscience. This is a perennial criticism of scholars involved in building a critical archaeology. In the pragmatist view, and all things being equal, science is an excellent model of human community and solidarity (Rorty 1991: 39). But unfortunately, all things are rarely equal. Where compromises are required, science is what must lead the way, since it has for too long (and as a consequence of unequal power relationships) dominated and silenced other ways of knowing (Zimmerman 1997). In his *Federalist Paper No. 10,* James Madison noted the threat to community presented by "majority factions." For Madison, the best corrective to the majoritarian threat was enlarging the scope of community, that is, the number of interests represented at the table of democracy. To the extent that mainstream, realist science is a majority faction in American archaeology, it poses the greatest threat to the project of reconciling competing knowledges and expanding community. Archaeologists and subaltern "others" alike tend to cringe at any call for compromise in the service of reconciliation and stronger community. But Rorty (1998: 52) provides some comfort when he reminds us that, in democratic societies, "you often get things done by compromising principles in order to form alliances with groups about whom you have grave doubts."

Summary

Pragmatism emphasizes ways of living instead of rules for knowing, the weaving together of knowledges instead of their validation against experience, and the social utility of narratives instead of the absolute truth of laws and theories. These governing ideals neither forsake reality nor undermine the possibilities for learning, nor do they capitulate to relativism in the way that term is usually understood. Pragmatism subsumes Enlightenment criterial rationality and nomothetics to more humanistic—but no less explicit and compelling—regulative ideals. In so doing, it converges with the epistemologies of subaltern groups—native peoples, working classes—for whom the social causes and consequences of scientific knowledge-claims can be of great concern. This in turn promises a more collaborative and democratic, and less authoritarian, archaeology.

At the same time, pragmatism usefully breaks with both the analytical (empiricist, positivist) and the continental (post-positivist) philosophical traditions that many have found wanting as underpinnings for contemporary archaeological practice. The desirable outcome of pragmatism's advocacy of these particular notions of truth, experience, and testing is stronger community—richer and better human activity—rather than some singular, final truth about the past or some imagined "more comprehensive" or "more complete" account of history. The loyalty in pragmatism is to other human beings struggling to cope rather than to the realist hope of getting things right; the desire is for solidarity rather than objectivity.

Pragmatist philosophy is thus fully compatible with the theoretical interests of an archaeology of collective action. It also meets those criteria enunciated by scholars seeking a more ethical practice (for example, contributors to Lynott and Wylie 2000). These include the need to be self-conscious of one's subjectivity, accountable for one's presuppositions and claims, and responsive to the various constituencies having an interest in the past. Pragmatism's ethical imperatives especially resonate with Martin Hall's (2004) redefinition of ethics as "principles of engagement" whereby we, as contributors to public knowledge, use our knowledge to serve the public good—whatever we take "public good" to mean.

Whether these ethical principles are best theorized as universal (good for all times and places) or situational (a matter of comparing time- and space-bound practices with each other) is subject to debate. I lean toward Rorty's (2001) position that community building is best served by situationalism or, in his terms, "ethnocentrism": that there is more to be gained by replacing the Enlightenment rationalist commitment to universal moral obligations with the rather more modest idea that we—as Westerners, intellectuals, archaeologists, or whatever—merely have some instructive and possibly persuasive stories to tell that might help to build trust across the boundaries that divide us from others. On this view, moral and ethical progress is viewed as an expansion in the number of people among whom unforced agreement can be established through free and open encounters (Rorty 1991).

Pragmatism's emphasis on narrative and conversation (Bernstein 1988) is perhaps its greatest offering to a discipline such as archaeology. Indeed, these commitments fit well with Ian Hodder's (1999: 19) view that archaeology today—given the diversity of theories, methods, and voices that have come to characterize it—is beginning to look less like a well-defined, bounded discipline and more like a fluid set of negotiated interactions. It is looking less like a "thing" than a "process." This community of discourses (Hodder 2001a: 3), while threatening what some might see as an unproductive dispersion of scientific energy, is mostly to the good if it stimulates imagination and experimentation and sustains intellectual vitality. In the next chapter, I discuss some of the ideas in theory and method that practitioners of critical archaeologies are using to produce better understandings of the past as well as better and stronger community.

Thinking and Tracking Collective Action
in Archaeological Contexts

This chapter covers basic theoretical and methodological issues in the archaeological study of collective action. It describes the theories of culture and material culture that inform the book's primary case study and delineates the methodological process by which these theories give meaning to archaeological data. I advocate a partitive theory of culture, a contextual theory of material culture, and an interpretive method for linking theory and data.

To clarify my position, I place these theoretical and methodological commitments in historical perspective by tracing their origins to critiques of earlier approaches. The development of these positions is largely conjoined: partitive theories of culture emerged at roughly the same time as contextual theories of material culture and interpretive methods. I do not mean to imply, however, that their emergence represents a distinct progressive stage in the maturation of archaeology as a scientific discipline (Preucel and Hodder 1996: 6). Although informed by the accumulation of new knowledge, these commitments are also the product of changing social contexts and sensibilities. They are indebted in significant ways to what came before and to old ideas that still have methodological and interpretive value.

Theory of Culture

How we conceive of culture—the metaphors and models that we use to structure inquiry and communicate results—significantly constrains and shapes our understanding of the past. In other words, these conceptions strongly inform the theoretical judgments that give meaning to archaeological data. In the preceding half century—when archaeology became less of an antiquarian and more of a scientific pursuit—archaeologists analyzed societies by focusing on cultural systems, human agents, and social collectives. Each entry point to analysis has merits, limitations, and consequences.

Cultural Systems

The cultural systems approach developed within the so-called new or processual archaeology that dominated the field during the 1960s and 1970s. Processualism was the first explicit attempt to transform archaeology into a scientific study of how cultures work and why they change. To do so, processual archaeology embraced the positivist philosophy characteristic of the natural sciences. Its ambitions were nomothetic and generalizing. From variability evident in the archaeological record, it sought to distill laws of culture process and evolutionary change that were good for all times and places. This marked a break from the older culture history paradigm, which favored a normative, particularistic view of culture as it existed in, and was shaped by, particular historical contexts. The scientific and evolutionary turn of American processual archaeology, like developments in other disciplines, was propelled by fears associated with the 1957 Sputnik launch and hopes associated with the 1959 Darwin centennial.

To fulfill its scientific ambitions, processual archaeology views societies through the machine-organism analogy of cultural systems: as tightly integrated, functional wholes that adapt to their environments. The different parts, or subsystems, of culture—for example, technology, social organization, ideology—work together to achieve adaptation. Indeed, culture itself is defined as the human organism's "extrasomatic means of adaptation" (Binford 1962: 218; see also White 1959). Cultures are viewed as problem-solving entities, with matter and energy exchanges—technoeconomic relationships—privileged as an entry point to analysis of the whole. Cultures vary as a function of resource structures and environmental carrying capacities, and they change in response to external, biophysical stimuli such as climate change and population-resource imbalances (see, for example, contributors to Hill 1977). This marks another break with culture history, which relied on historical events such as population migration and the cross-cultural spread or diffusion of ideas as explanations for why cultures change over time. Again, wider societal conditions likely shaped processual archaeology's view of causality. The processual paradigm developed at the same time that Rachel Carson's *Silent Spring* (1962) put environmental problems on society's radar screen, and Paul Ehrlich's *Population Bomb* (1968) raised concerns about runaway demographic growth and impending imbalances between people and resources. Both works had wide populist appeal in the 1960s and 1970s (Trigger 1981; Patterson 1986).

Although the architects of processual archaeology recognized that people differentially participate in culture (Binford 1962), the dynamics internal to the cultural system are held constant. Cowgill (1975: 506, cited in Brumfiel 1992:

552) noted that systems theorists have no interest in "the needs, problems, possibilities, incentives, information, and viewpoints of specific individuals or categories of individuals" within the system. In keeping with cybernetic metaphors, cultural systems are assumed to be in equilibrium until something knocks them out of kilter. And, like the specific content of cultural systems, the specifics of local histories are also deemed to be relatively unimportant. The details of local history are useful only to the extent that they can help distill lawlike generalizations about culture and cultural change writ large.

Processual archaeology was useful in sensitizing archaeologists to cultural variation, the interconnectedness of social and environmental variables, and causation that was more structural and less idiosyncratic (Brumfiel 1992). Its explicit focus on culture-environment ("man-land") relationships positioned the discipline for many theoretical and methodological breakthroughs in the study of energy and matter exchanges. Among the important developments were settlement catchment analysis, optimal foraging theory, and a host of data recovery methods that increased the resolution of our picture of the past. Perhaps most important is that processualism funded an optimism about what could be known about the world through archaeology. This in turn produced a list of advances in what Hill (1991) terms "descriptive" and "explanatory" knowledge. Processual analyses also produced an understanding of long-term patterns that could inform predictions about how cultural systems were likely to perform under various environmental conditions.

But at the same time, the cultural systems approach has not delivered laws of cultural change akin to those produced in the natural sciences. As new methods and accumulating data improved the precision with which we could know the past, they exposed complexity in how cultures work and change. By the late 1970s, the presumed driving variables of environment, climate, and population had begun to look suspect. This suggested that something else was involved in culture change: either different external variables or the internal variables of social organization and ideology that mediated and thereby complicated how people dealt with exogenous forces.

The intellectual unrest within archaeology was reinforced by wider developments in cultural and academic life. The deepening social and economic crises of the late 1970s exposed flaws in the cybernetic concepts of stability, continuity, and equilibrium that informed systems theory (Patterson 1986). At the same time, the humanities, social sciences, and even some parts of the natural sciences began undergoing a postmodern turn that challenged the utility of "grand" or "master" narratives about the past and their accompanying positivist epistemologies. These were seen as flattening or homogenizing past societies (Funari, Hall, and Jones 1999). Instead, enthusiasm was gathering for experimentation with smaller narratives focused on everyday life and the lived experience of people contained by the cultural system. A high value was placed on theoretical pluralism. This aided and abetted an emerging indigenous peoples' activism and informed the first stirrings of "dialogical" or "covenantal" archaeologies (Zimmerman 1997). These archaeologies questioned the utility of gathering generalized information about human societies at the expense of more specific, local knowledge (Gosden 2001).

Human Agents

This intellectual unrest crystallized in the late 1970s and early 1980s with the formation of a new framework for archaeological inquiry, what has been variously described as postprocessual, contextual, or interpretive archaeology (Johnson 1999). This approach replaces the cultural system with a focus on the individual human agent, an orientation that still informs much archaeological theorizing.

Early postprocessual critics indicted processualism's denial of the active role of individuals in social life and change in a variety of ways. Binford's claim about the differential participation of people in culture notwithstanding, systems theory reduced individual social actors to "invisible, equivalent, abstract units" (Brumfiel 1992: 552). Individuals shared a fundamental sameness in their material conditions of existence (Hodder 1982a; Tilley 1982; Paynter 1989; Marquardt 1992). Actors accepted and played by the same set of rules and for the same kinds of adaptive goals (Braun 1991). Individuals were "shuffled around from one adaptive state to the next" (Tilley 1989: 109). Processualism reinforced an uncritical behaviorism that often cast individuals as maze-bound rats who instinctively responded to external stimuli (Wobst 2000). Tringham (1991: 94) famously expressed a frustration with processual theory that represented people as "faceless blobs." A critique framed in somewhat kinder terms charged processualism with reducing people to passive carriers of culture, rather than respecting them as active creators of culture (Paynter 1989).

Anticipating what would become a crucial variable in the agent-centered approach, some critics exposed what they saw as the "vulgar" ideological bias of systems theory; that is, a bias that patently serves the interests of a particular social class (Meltzer 1981). The machine-organism analogy of systems theory was identified as the natural ideology of bureaucratic planners and centralizers, one predicated on the priority of social control (Patterson 1986). On this understanding, that processual archaeology developed when it did is not surprising. Its formative context is one in which the American social order was being threatened by war, energy shortages, and conflicts over civil rights—all classic middle-class concerns (Trigger 1981, 1986; Patterson 1986). Indeed, when actors in systems theories were identified, they tended to be elites who, in keeping with archaeology's traditional status as a middle-class pursuit, performed managerial functions that would lead society to a new adaptive equilibrium. The rise of the state, for example, correlated with and depended on the rise of a managerial middle class (McGuire and Walker 1999: 163).

This lack of attention to individual agents and their myriad entanglements within a cultural system in turn meant that processual archaeology could contribute very little to a theory of internally generated social change. Disinterest in the partitive relationships that could create difference and disjuncture—unequal social relationships or different ideologies—also deprived analysts of ways to explain the lack of fit between processual theory's expectations and the empirical record. For other critics, the failure to consider social and ideological relationships—as well as the specific, contingent details of local histories—spiritually removed archaeologists from their subjects of inquiry. At worst processualism dehumanized indigenous peoples; at best it cultivated a narrow and restricted view of behavior that avoided topics of great interest to both native people and the general public (Trigger 1980, 1986: 205–6).

Alternatively, agency approaches work with different ontologies (for reviews see Dobres and Robb 2000; Dornan 2002). People are put back into culture, along with the cognitive factors—for example, the meaning frameworks by which people assign significance to events and things—that inform and motivate their actions. Agency approaches are broadly concerned with the conscious, creative activities of individuals within limits established by historically specific social structures and cultural values. Postprocessualism reunited society with history (Patterson 1986) and in so doing rediscovered a key insight of the older culture history approach. It was keenly interested in the particulars of local historical context—the roles played by historically contingent events in shaping culture—for their own sake, rather than as fodder for building sweeping evolutionary narratives driven by cultural laws.

Theoretical work by Bourdieu (1977) and Giddens (1979, 1984) provides the intellectual warrant for exploring what postprocessualists see as a reflexive, recursive, or dialectical relationship between agency and structure in historical context. Among the social relationships or structuring principles highlighted for analysis by postprocessual archaeologists are those involving gender, age, ethnicity, and other identities. Empirical work documents the causal efficacy of the relationship between these structuring principles and human action (contributors to Hodder 1982a; Miller and Tilley 1984a; McGuire and Paynter

1991; Gero and Conkey 1991). These structures organize human action and are reproduced in the practices of everyday life. Research into the everyday functioning of such relationships indicates that change in these domains of life occurs on a temporal scale visible to the participants in a culture. That is, the changes are accessible to human consciousness (Paynter and McGuire 1991). Moreover, these principles significantly shape societal responses to the phenomena that concern processualists, such as environmental change (Paynter and McGuire 1991).

Social power is of particular interest to agency approaches. Power serves as the major touchstone for considering the operation of structuring relationships around gender, age, ethnicity, and class. Drawing on work by Foucault (1979, 1980) and others, agency theories start with the assumption that all societies are predicated on power differences and conflicts of interests among individuals (Rowlands 1982: 168; Tilley 1982: 36, 1984: 114; Miller and Tilley 1984b; Miller, Rowlands, and Tilley 1989; Paynter 1989; Paynter and McGuire 1991). The operative notion of power in these approaches is complex, however. Power is not viewed as a unitary thing or quantity that is doled out in society. Rather, it is seen as a property of all social relationships (Miller and Tilley 1984b; Paynter and McGuire 1991). All people have access to practical power, or *power to,* defined as the capacity to intervene in events to alter them. Fewer people have access to *power over,* the power that comes with control of strategic resources and life chances, which in turn forms the basis of social domination (Miller and Tilley 1984b). But even domination is accompanied by resistance: the ability to challenge or subvert relations of "power over." Both domination and resistance are viewed as heterogeneous. They take a multiplicity of forms and are expressed at a variety of institutional sites in society (for example, household, school, workplace, state), as well as at a variety of spatial scales (Wolf 1990; Marquardt 1992).

As noted above, the concept of ideology is also crucial to this understanding of social power and its contestation. Ideology is a set of ideas about nature, cause, time, and person—those things that are taken by society as a given (Leone 1984). It is understood as a framework of meaning within which resources and objects are given value, inequalities are defined, and power is legitimated or challenged (Hodder and Hutson 2003). In this view, ideology is indispensable to sustaining or impeding the efficient operation of power in contexts where power relations are tenuous and challengeable. Drawing on theoretical work by Giddens, postprocessualists theorize ideology as functioning to legitimize inequalities in at least three ways: naturalizing them by rooting them in the external world; universalizing them by showing their widespreadedness and/or timelessness; or denying that inequalities exist by masking them from view. As will be established below, material culture is seen as crucial to ideology's legitimizing project.

Social Collectives

Like system theories, agency theories proved useful in moving archaeology in new and productive directions. They got us thinking about the freedom or relative autonomy that individuals have to move within structures, and about ideas instead of just material conditions. Students working with Ian Hodder at Cambridge and Mark Leone at Maryland produced interesting accounts of the past that linked the material and the ideal in new and exciting ways on both sides of the ancient/modern divide (Johnson 1999). In time, agency critiques and original empirical work forced processualism to respond. Many organizing concepts of postprocessualism were subsequently incorporated into an array of approaches in North American archaeology, one that Hegmon (2003) describes as "processual-plus" (see also Pauketat's [2001] "historical processualism").

It was only a matter of time, however, before the concept of human agency would come under fire, just as the notion of human behavior had before that. Critiques of agency start with the observation that individual agency is but one particular form of agency (Johnson 1989; Hodder and Hutson 2003). Thomas (2000), drawing on Foucault's theoretical formulations, notes that the idea of the autonomous individual exercising rational choice and free will is a relatively recent invention, specific to modernity. He argues that humans always carry out their projects in the context of a concrete material world that includes other people and that considering human beings in abstraction from the relationships in which they find themselves is insufficient. Barrett (2001) agrees, noting that agency must also include the operation of social collectives that extend beyond the individual's body and lifespan. Hodder (2004) suggests that agency, like power, is less a thing we possess than a capacity that we exercise. With Thomas, he sees the group as forming part of the resources used for individual agency, and he thus views group behavior as another form of individual agency (also see Hodder and Hutson 2003: 104).

McGuire and Wurst (2002) push the critique of agency theory the furthest. They argue that theories of individual agency in postprocessual archaeology are just as "vulgarly" ideological as the cultural systems theories that preceded them. Specifically, they identify the focus on the individual agent as a sustaining belief of modern capitalism (Marx 1963; Eagleton 1996). Capitalism depends for its survival on cultural processes that constitute people as free and unfettered individuals, and thus it works, through its cultural forms, to universalize this historically contingent idea. Where this ideology is internalized and taken-for-granted, it obscures the oppositional nature of class groupings and exploitation in society. It also produces the kind of self-serving identity politics that can fragment and debilitate collective movements for change. Thus, McGuire and Wurst (2002) find advocacy of individual agency models by scholars intending to use their research to challenge class, gender, and racial inequalities in the modern world to be misguided and contradictory. By embracing the logic, language, and symbolism of individual agency, activist scholars are in fact reinforcing that which they wish to critique. By projecting and universalizing that which is contingent, they help to propagate existing social relations. This is a notion of agency that lacks transformative, emancipatory, and revolutionary potential (Harvey 1973).

Alternatively, McGuire and Wurst (2002) see individuals as always thoroughly enmeshed in a web of social relations. Collective action results from the shared consciousness or solidarity that defines a community of individual agents. Such consciousness may be based in class, gender, ethnicity, race, or some combination of these identities. People make history as members of social groups whose common consciousness derives from shared existential anxieties, political interests, and social relations. To the extent that these anxieties, interests, and relations are traceable to larger forces like global capitalism, and to the extent that community is always a delicate relation between fluid processes of self-identification and relatively permanent associations like that between person and nation-state (Harvey 2000: 240), archaeology needs grand narratives of the structural and long term as well as small narratives of lived moments (Hodder 1999: 147).

In summary, the critiques of agency by Thomas, Hodder, and McGuire and Wurst usefully respond to Orser's (2003: 131) worry that agency has become an "all inclusive buzzword" for archaeologists, covering so many diverse human actions that it is "rapidly acquiring non-meaning." These critiques link up with Fabian's point, discussed in chapter 2, that human acting is always acting in company. The task today is to sort out and better theorize agency's many dimensions (Hodder 2004: 32; Dobres and Robb 2005). We need to analyze the broad relationships that produce agents with particular subjectivities and study the social processes used within particular groups to negotiate and coordinate group behavior and consensus (Hodder 2004: 32). This will be so much the better for identifying those subjectivities and collectivities from the past that might have relevance for political action in the present.

Theory of Material Culture

Tracking the action of cultural systems, individual human agents, and social collectives in the past depends on particular understandings of material culture. There is now a rich and expanding literature that deals with *materiality*: how the things we make and use—broadly understood to include everything from mundane portable objects to monumental buildings to entire built landscapes—influence the way we act, express ourselves, and give meaning to our lives (Meskell and Preucel 2004b). Many scholars have established how people are socialized within and through the material world. Some see objects as political or tactical weapons—as themselves having agency (for example, Gell 1998). Material culture—to the extent that it is meaning-loaded in ways that go beyond an object's physical properties—is an active part of human existence. There is a spreading appreciation that archaeology's ability to understand how individuals and collectives creatively use the material world to establish and further their interests is the most significant contribution that the discipline can make to contemporary intellectual life (see, for example, contributors to Meskell and Preucel 2004a).

This understanding of material culture was a long time in coming. Over the years, anthropologists and archaeologists have dealt with material culture in many ways. Ontologies of material culture have moved from viewing objects as *signs for* culture, to objects as providing *information about* culture, to the recent appreciation of objects as *constitutive of* culture. As with changes in theories of society, changes in theories of material culture are as much a product of changing social contexts and sensibilities as accumulating knowledge.

The Object as a "Sign for" Culture

The earliest theories of material culture understood objects as a straightforward reflection of a culture's place in a hierarchical, unilinear arrangement of evolutionary stages. Cultural evolutionism was the first influential grand narrative in anthropology, classifying cultures into savagery, barbarism, and civilization (Morgan 1877). Material culture served as an important basis for this categorization. Objects exemplified, or stood for, a cultural stage. Hunting and gathering technologies (for example, bow and arrow) typified savagery, agricultural technologies (for example, pottery) reflected barbarism, and our own industrial technologies indicated civilization. Cultural evolution saw an isomorphic association between people and objects (Buchli 2004: 180). The view of culture was essentialist and progressivist; the meaning of objects was fixed and static. Today we see this view as deeply flawed because of the great diversity and overlap in material forms that are observable across cultures and time periods and because of the narrative's unselfconscious ethnocentrism. But cultural evolutionism was useful in its day for identifying a general pattern of variation that could allow cross-cultural comparison. It also established the study of non-Western cultures as a legitimate scholarly pursuit.

In the first half of the twentieth century, anthropology responded to the worst excesses and biases of cultural evolutionism. Scholars such as Franz Boas were alert to the disturbing consequences of "progress" as then defined: war, poverty, and a general increase in human misery. Boasians challenged the equation of people with stage in a unilinear, hierarchical ranking of cultural achievement. As a result of this critique, anthropology and archaeology turned to the detailed description and analysis of particular cultures in historical context: the paradigm of culture history. But culture history pretty much reproduced cultural evolutionism's understanding of material culture. The view of material culture, like that of culture itself, was normative and idealist. Objects were seen to be expressions of abstract rules or mental templates about how to behave. Differences in the form of objects across space were attributed to cultural learning, and the amount of formal variation in a single place was attributed to population movements or interaction frequency with people in other places.

Instead of using objects to pigeonhole cultures into stages of development, culture historians used them to better define a culture's location in space and time. But culture history's normative conception of culture and its limited concern for artifact variability in a particular place implicated a view of cultural actors as largely imitative and minimally creative (Trigger 1980, 1986). This in turn limited what could be learned about the internal dynamics of culture and the causes of change over time. Cultural anthropologists of the day picked up on this limitation and often disparaged archaeology as the "lesser part" of anthropology (see also Conkey 1989).

The Object as Providing "Information about" Culture

The emergence of processual archaeology marked a breakthrough in the study of material culture. As discussed above, processual archaeologists were interested in cultural process and change. For processualists there were no inherent limitations to the study of material culture as a way to learn about the past. Rather, the problem was a dearth of theory for dealing with objects.

Binford's seminal paper "Archaeology as Anthropology" (1962) set the tone for an entire generation of young scholars. In keeping with the systemic view of culture as humankind's extrasomatic means of adaptation, Binford argued that objects could provide information about a whole gamut of adaptive practices from subsistence to ideology. He proposed a set of important concepts for classifying material culture. *Technomic* objects—tools—were those that had their primary functional context in coping directly with the material environment. *Sociotechnic* objects—a king's crown, a chief's feather cloak—had their primary functional role in organizing a cohesive group so that technology could be efficiently manipulated. *Ideotechnic* objects—clan symbols, deity figures—signified and symbolized ideological rationalizations for the cultural system and acculturated people into it.

This view of material culture led to much subsequent research on artifact variation and function but did not address such questions as why artifacts took the forms that they did or functioned in the ways that they did. Explanatory reference was to adaptive functional contexts rather than to historical circumstances. The professed interest in ideology notwithstanding, processual archaeology started with technoenvironmental relationships and basically ended there. As connoted by Binford's own terms for describing artifact variety, technology was prioritized as that aspect of life about which we can best learn. Objects were seen to be reflective of technological, social, and ideological realms of life, rather than fully constitutive of those realms.

Dobres (2000) shows what this view of objects came to in her study of the visual representations used in scientific and popular writing of the time. Prehistoric tools were often pictured as held by disembodied hands. Where photos and museum dioramas included full-body human agents, the images were desocialized. A lone toolmaker was shown surrounded by debitage, or men and women were shown working at different tasks. Even members of the same sex involved in the same activity were rarely shown interacting with or even acknowledging each other. Instead, people were concentrating on the particular task at hand. In such representations, culture is, literally, all work and no play. The visual tropes of processual archaeology suggest that there was lots of adapting going on in past cultural systems but much less conscious and purposeful creating.

The Object as "Constitutive of" Culture

The late 1970s and early 1980s postprocessual turn toward more nuanced, partitive conflict views of social process, and to questions of cultural meaning, produced interest in the other kinds of work that objects can do. The result was the emergence of a contextual theory of material culture in which agents and objects both actively work to create culture (Conkey 1989). Objects are not simply reflective of evolutionary stage, time/space provenance, or adaptive state but are actively constitutive of social relations. They are used in political and ideological struggles between contesting groups and are often given new meanings that challenge the old as they move between social contexts. Objects "push back," advancing and constraining human action in ways informed by local circumstances and history. Indeed, in this view, objects *are* culture (Conkey 1989).

This new view was pioneered by scholars working across the spectrum and with varying degrees of commitment to processualism. Martin Wobst (1977) proposed, within a largely processual paradigm, a notion of style as a means of communication, that is, as information exchange about ethnic identity, political affiliation, and emotional state. Wobst saw artifact style as a "pleasantly multidimensional and surprisingly dynamic" phenomenon (1977: 335), not something that was applied by a Skinnerian automaton and whose meaning and function were given before application. His article "Stylistic Behavior and Information Exchange" is a tour de force in alerting archaeologists to the ways in which artifact style can function strategically to ease social interaction between people. Using examples from the ethnically diverse and conflict-latent former Yugoslavia, Wobst developed baseline expectations for the kinds of objects that should carry information, the kinds of groups at which object messages should be targeted, and the kinds of social contexts within which objects carrying information should circulate. Wobst also offered up several counterintuitive implications of stylistic behavior that would never have occurred to culture historians, for example, that stylistically loaded but short-lived objects are not necessarily "fashion failures" if they accomplish a social purpose, and that stylistic elaboration of the material world can be an indicator of a society that is in trouble, rather than one that is harmoniously functioning. Today Wobst continues to do innovative theorizing about object form, offering cogent arguments for distinguishing between human behavior and human action, and why we need more efforts in relating objects to the latter (Wobst 2000). His notion of objects as material interferences (see chapter 1) is embedded in the interpretive theories that orient the case studies discussed in this book.

Ian Hodder (1982c) played off of Wobst's work in developing a view of material culture that saw all objects, not just a Wobstian subset, as "symbols in action" strategically used within human power relations. Like Wobst, Hodder drew upon ethnographic societies for illustrative material. He analyzed how, in the Baringo area of East Africa, spear and calabash styles were used by young men and women, respectively, to challenge the political and economic dominance of older men. Both groups shared a common predicament vis-à-vis senior males, who sought to control their labor and life chances. In one study, Hodder (1991b) examined how a "V" design on calabash containers mirrored the "V" design painted on the chests of young, unmarried warriors. Hodder interpreted this association as a conscious attempt by women to show solidarity with younger men in an effort to remind elders of the latent power of this social alliance. This is a lovely example of women working in the interstices of male power to advance their collective interest. It is also a nice example of alliance building across gender lines to engage with a generational power struggle. Hodder, with Wobst, clearly breaks with culture history in showing that style is not simply a reflection of rote human learning or inter-group interaction frequency.

At the same time, Mark Leone (1984, 1986) was moving in similarly creative directions in historical archaeology. Leone used the critical theory of Haber-mas (1971) in conjunction with historical documents to interpret artifacts in early colonial Annapolis as ideological. The key idea underpinning the study of ideology with objects is the notion that meaning is not merely something that is found in peoples' heads. Rather, it is material and public and is repro-duced in the practices of everyday life (Roseberry 1989; Hodder 1991c; Hodder and Hutson 2003). Leone's specific studies of Annapolis give us a view of how mid-eighteenth-century Maryland elites, increasingly alienated from their fel-low elites in England and increasingly separated by wealth and power from working classes in the colonies, produced and popularized particular kinds of material landscapes, buildings, and object assemblages to "convince people that a rational social order based in nature was possible and that those with ac-cess to its laws were natural leaders" (Leone 1988: 250). His seminal analysis of William Paca's Garden (Leone 1984) showed how principles of order and rules of perspective in landscape design were applied to make these built spaces ap-pear larger and more impressive, with symmetrical arrangements of classical statuary and terraces serving to ground the concept of ordered hierarchy in history and nature. Leone's chapter coauthored by Paul Shackel (1987) is a clas-sic study of how a variety of more mundane objects—forks, clocks, musical and scientific instruments—also functioned to sustain and reproduce power differences. Such objects helped create the individual subjectivities and be-haviors conducive to an emerging capitalist work discipline and thus further justified the existence of atomistic and hierarchical relationships in society. This work demonstrates how historical archaeologists can explore the contin-gent historical origins of that key construct—the individual agent—that some agency theorists cast as the default form of subjectivity for all cultures across time and space. Although Leone's work has been criticized for implicating nonelites as passive dupes in ideological power plays (Beaudry, Cook, and Mrozowski 1991; Orser 1996), it succeeds in showing how all artifacts—even those that processualism defines as technomic—are capable of doing social and ideological work.

In summary, the earliest evolutionary and culture history paradigms saw material culture as passive, as a static "sign for" evolutionary stage or time/ space provenance. In processual archaeology, material culture serves to provide "information about" different aspects of cultural systems and their overall adaptive state. In postprocessual archaeology, objects become fully "constitutive of" culture. Today, a contextual view of material culture is relatively commonplace. It has been taken on board by a number of archaeological approaches (for example, see contributors to Hodder 2001b; Hegmon 2003), and nicely serves the interpretive ambitions of this book. In the next section, I clarify the methodological process by which these theories of culture and material culture are used to give meaning to archaeological data.

Reading the Past

Having theories about the social and material worlds is one thing. Deploying these theories of culture and material culture in a way that gives meaning to the static, mute world of archaeological objects is another. There has been much debate about how to move from social theory to archaeological data in a coherent, controlled manner that fosters learning, especially learning that serves an emancipatory interest in the past's otherness.

Processualists committed to positivist epistemology have long advocated for development of a distinctive middle-range theory for accomplishing such learning (for example, Binford 1987). Middle-range theory is envisioned as a body of uniformitarian principles about behavior and its material effects that can guide interpretation so that we avoid unreflective and viciously circular impositions of theoretical preconceptions on archaeological data. Processualism's critics, influenced by the postmodern/postpositivist turn in philosophy, have argued that middle-range theory is illusory, since all analytical methods are inevitably metaphysically loaded. All data used to test or otherwise evaluate a theory have, in a fundamental way, already been constituted by the theory being tested and evaluated. Thus, no observation can be theory-neutral (Kosso 1991; Tschauner 1996).

This point about the theory-laden-ness of all observation has been well established by postpositivist philosophers. Consequently, Hodder (2004: 28) and other postprocessualists have convincingly argued that archaeology is not an experimental science best furthered by hypothetico-deductive encounters with data as mediated by independent middle range theory, but rather is a historical science powered by interpretation. Postprocessualism uses the concept of "reading" the past to describe this interpretive process. Reading the past depends upon a dialectical, recursive, back-and-forth movement between theory and data, between ideas about human sociality and the archaeological record's materiality. Hodder (2004) also describes this interpretive method as *hermeneutical*. And because the material we study has also been shaped by the meaning frameworks used by the ancestors, archaeological interpretation involves a *double hermeneutic* that defies hypothesis testing as it is conventionally understood (Preucel and Hodder 1996: 13). Interpretation involves fitting together multiple lines of evidence to produce a coherent and compelling account of the past. We then evaluate different interpretations in terms of their ability to account for all available relevant evidence, their logical coherence, their fruitfulness for raising new questions and opening up new lines of inquiry, and their wider social relevance and impacts (Hodder 1999: 59–62; Hodder and Hutson 2003).

This interpretive and evaluative approach dovetails with the pragmatist view of science detailed in chapter 2. There, the metaphor of "weaving together" was advocated as a way to engage descendant community understandings of the past to better ascertain and learn from the past's otherness. The same sort of metaphor serves to usefully describe engagements with archaeological data. Indeed, one can argue that hermeneutic fitting or pragmatic weaving is what all archaeologists do. Similarly, Wylie (1993) characterizes the interpretive process as one of tacking between multiple lines of evidence that, taken together, impose decisive empirical constraints on what we can reasonably accept as a plausible account of the past. Many archaeologists across the paradigmatic spectrum have been speaking of a reflexive back-and-forth movement between theory and data (Watson 1986; Sabloff, Binford, and McAnany 1987; Dunnell 1989: 36; Whitley 1992: 58–59; Tschauner 1996). These accounts of archaeological interpretation even harmonize with Geertz's (1983) notion of "dialectical tacking" between parts and whole as a way to interpret ethnographic cultures. Thus, they capture what for many scholars is unavoidably common anthropological practice.

Today many concepts and ideas exist for guiding movement between theory and data in ways that can produce new understandings of human agency in the past (Dobres and Robb 2005). Starting from a conviction that archaeology can provide access to the "full theatre" of domination and resistance, Paynter and McGuire (1991) bring together ideas about how power relations can be tracked in both tribal and industrial capitalist social orders by analyzing a variety of object categories. They note that the key challenge for politically dominant groups is to get the oppressed to participate in their own oppression, given the costliness of using coercive force to maintain structures of inequality. Elites have employed everything from pots to pyramids, forks to fortresses to accomplish this. Alternatively, the challenge for the oppressed is to resist domination in ways that do not risk reprisals, that is, to "cover their tracks" (Scott 1985: 278–84). It is reasonable to expect such resistance to show up in private and public contexts via the information-coding potential of material culture.

Elsewhere I have summarized some ideas for tracking specifically class relations of surplus extraction and distribution that can inform theories of collective action (Saitta 1992; see also Paynter 1988 for earlier work in this direction). Variation over space and time in ratios of public to private storage, densities of exotics exchange, degrees of labor investment in fixed material culture, and the formal geometry of built environments at different spatial scales are all lines of evidence that can speak to political and economic struggles over surplus flow and accompanying struggles over flows of cultural meaning. No single line of evidence is an unambiguous guide to such class dynamics. Rather, the best strategy—as articulated by Hodder—is to play one line of evidence off against a multiplicity of others. Discrepancies between actual empirical patterns and governing theory are to be expected. The application of new theory and, especially, imagination to the study of discrepancies can implicate novel organizational realities and dynamics for past societies, thereby contributing to learning and furthering the development of general social theory. Approached in this way, the problem of vicious circularity in interpretation and the risk of masking past organizational variability is minimized (see also Tringham 1991).

Summary

This chapter has covered some of the key theoretical and methodological ideas that inform an archaeology of collective action, including their intellectual roots and contemporary context. These ideas include a partitive theory of culture, a contextual theory of material culture, and an interpretive method for giving meaning to archaeological data. In the next chapter, I consider how these and other ideas for investigating agency in the past come together in particular case studies of race-, gender-, and class-based collective action.

Archaeologies of Collective Action

Historical archaeologists have made important breakthroughs in our understanding of collective action in the past. Paynter (2000b) offers a comprehensive review of the existing literature. Race-, gender-, and class-based forms of collective action have also been considered (see, for example, contributors to Leone and Potter 1988, 1999; McGuire and Paynter 1991; Scott 1994; Delle, Mrozowski, and Paynter 2000a; Van Bueren 2002; Hall and Silliman 2006a). This chapter highlights a few of these studies as a way to illustrate the merging of theory and data discussed in the previous chapter and as a segue into the extended case study that follows.

Several shared assumptions about race, gender, and class identity guide studies of past collective action. In all cases, identities are understood to be multiple, fluid, and situational. They are seen to be intertwined and thus difficult to study in isolation from each other. In other words, identities are constituted relationally (Meskell and Preucel 2004d). Brubaker and Cooper (2000) have critiqued this "soft," constructivist view of identity, arguing that it can allow any number of putative identities to proliferate, empty the term of meaning, and thereby lose analytical purchase on the world. They are equally critical of stronger, categorical views that fix and essentialize identity and thus inform the sort of identity politics critiqued by McGuire and Wurst (2002). Brubaker and Cooper instead argue for the use of alternative terms, such as *identification* and *self-understanding*. Here, I stick with the relational view while remaining cognizant of the fact that all conceptions of the world have merits and liabilities as entry points for critical analysis and social change (Saitta 2005).

This chapter's presentation is necessarily selective. The inclusion of a case study depends on that work's success in demonstrating how shared existential anxiety and identity produced specific collective strategies for achieving change and its relevance as a comparative touchstone for the Colorado case study discussed in chapters 5 and 6. Because of the interpenetrability of race, class, and gender, assignment of a study to a particular category is in some cases arbitrary. All of these studies, however, are illustrative of what is possible with an archaeology attuned to collective action.

Race

African diaspora studies provide a rich source of insights about race-based collective action in the past. Much discussion and debate has swirled around the existence and meaning of "Africanisms"—objects that either have a clear connection to African cultural practice or show significant commonalities among African diaspora communities—in the New World (Mullins 2004). Today, there is a spreading recognition that a search for Africanisms is unproductive if it invests objects with a static identity or reinforces a monolithic view of African culture (Orser 1998). Alternatively, such artifacts are best viewed relationally—as having fluid meanings dependent on context that conceivably reference something in addition to, and even other than, African culture. That is, they are best seen as Hodderian "symbols in action"—as active representations of otherness manipulated by individuals and groups within power relations (Singleton 1995; Orser 1998).

Singleton (2005) summarizes important work by Lorena Walsh and Patricia Samford that implicates slave collective agency in the Chesapeake region. Walsh shows that at Utopia Plantation in Virginia, slaves built housing using Anglo-Virginian carpentry techniques but used African ideas of domestic space in placing houses in a square formation around an open courtyard. These courtyards would have provided central places for cooking and socializing. Singleton also reviews interesting studies of the rectangular and square subfloor pits that were dug within slave houses. Samford resists functional interpretations that relate pits to storage or to the concealment of pilfered items. Instead, she favors a ritual interpretation. Using accounts of West African Igbo and Yoruba religious practices, Samford suggests that these pits served as household shrines used to bury religious items. Singleton notes that the existence of these pits often produced conflict between slaveholders and slave laborers. They served to challenge slaveholder control over living spaces. As we see in chapter 6, immigrant workers at the Ludlow tent colony also used the arrangement of living spaces and features dug within them as tactics of resistance.

The most famous examples of slave collective agency are associated with colonoware pottery studies. Colonoware is a low-fired, unglazed, hand-built, and locally made earthenware found on African-American sites in the eighteenth century. Colonoware vessels were used for preparing, serving, and storing food. They are found in shapes that resemble both European and African forms. A long debate about who made colonoware has been resolved in favor of production by a number of groups, including Native Americans (Orser 1996: 117–23). The colonoware vessel is an "intercultural artifact" (Singleton and Bograd 2000: 8). Thus, interpretation needs to respect not only the form of these objects but also the geographical area where they are found and the relational context in which they are used.

Working in the South Carolina Lowcountry, Leland Ferguson (1991, 1992) offers the most compelling case for colonoware vessels as instruments of slave agency geared toward collective resistance. Colonoware is found in particular abundance on Lowcountry sites, especially those associated with slaves. Ferguson documents, via quantitative and qualitative analysis, that colonoware in this region connected slave foodways to West African precedents. He convincingly shows that the forms of colonoware vessels recall West African patterns. A high frequency of bowls and a bimodal size distribution of jars reflect the West African tradition of serving starches in larger vessels and sauces or relishes in smaller ones. Bowls and jars both have rounded bases, distinguishing them from Anglo-European flat and tripodal bases. Another contrast with European dining practices of the time lies in the fact that the vast majority of colonoware containers (98 percent of the sample studied by Ferguson) lack cutlery marks.

Thus, Lowcountry slaves were apparently eating like their African ancestors rather than their European masters and by extension were using foodways to build community. Additional support for an African ethos comes from evidence indicating that colonoware pots—like Samford's Chesapeake pits—functioned in slave religious practices. A small number of colonoware bowls have features that recall a generalized West African Bakongo religious iconography. Bakongo refers to a "generalized cultural expression" that crosscuts ethnic differences in the Congo-Angola region of Africa, where about 40 percent of South Carolina slaves originated (Ferguson 1999: 118). The iconographic features, or "cosmograms," include rounded ring bases and cross and circle designs incised into the pot's surface. In Bakongo culture, clay pots are used in renewal rituals as containers for medicines and charms, and the cross and circle symbolize harmony with the universe and the continuity of life. Interestingly, in the South Carolina Lowcountry, colonoware pots are often excavated in streamside and river bottom contexts. In Bakongo cosmology, water is associated with the separation between the living and spirit worlds. The water context association combined with their form and markings reinforces the interpretation of certain colonoware pots as "magic bowls" employed in community ritual.

Several lines of material evidence along with historical analysis of Bakongo cosmology and oral testimony from a twentieth-century Georgia healer (see Ferguson 1999) thus converge to make a compelling case that the production and distribution of colonoware pottery served slave collective agency. Such agency is also evident in Lowcountry house forms, even more so than in the Chesapeake (Singleton 2005). Slaves having different ethnic roots in Africa used material objects to help build a creolized subculture that blended African cultural elements with other elements and, at the same time, distanced this subaltern culture from the dominant Anglo-European rationalizations that supported the planter social order. To the extent that no status differences or other boundaries are reflected within the colonoware assemblage, slaves were nurturing reciprocity and community. In short, material culture was used to build and support a pan-African sense of syncretic culture among the diverse peoples enslaved in the South Carolina Lowcountry (Orser 1998; Ferguson 1999).

Finally, work by Paul Mullins (1999a) on African-American use of material goods after emancipation in Annapolis explores change over time in how segments of this population expressed their collective identity by reinterpreting artifacts associated with genteel white consumer culture. Between 1850 and 1930, emancipated African-Americans acquired previously inaccessible mass-produced parlor goods that were symbolically charged representations of American abundance and nationalism, signaling their owner's affluence and belonging (Orser 1998). These knickknacks were used by whites to materialize and naturalize white privilege and to justify discrimination against blacks (Brumfiel 2003). On Mullins's view, emancipated blacks procured these items to articulate their aspirations for full citizenship in a capitalist, consumer-oriented society. These objects do not indicate a desire to assimilate. Blacks gave the objects new meanings in the interest of combating old racist notions of black material inferiority, distancing themselves from old racist caricatures generally, and negotiating expanded space for themselves in a new national order (Orser 1998).

Gender

Scholars researching gender have long been at the forefront of efforts to produce more nuanced understandings of social power relationships and organizational change. Paralleling historical archaeology's initial interest in documenting the slave presence through the search for Africanisms, early work in the archaeology of gender was dedicated to making women's lives more visible, to "finding women" in the archaeological record. Later work became more fully relational, studying how women and men interacted in divisions of labor and other social arrangements (contributors to Gero and Conkey 1991). Today, there is an impressive diversity of theoretical standpoints and research questions among archaeologists concerned with gender (Dobres and Robb 2000; Paynter 2000b). This has led to important breakthroughs in our understanding of gender roles and strategies in the past.

Spencer-Wood's (1991, 1994, 2003) research on nineteenth- and early-twentieth-century "domestic reform" sites in Boston and elsewhere explores strategies by which female domestic reformers sought to improve the conditions of women's lives by expanding their roles in both private and public spaces. She illustrates how reformers used the material world to accomplish this goal. Reformers employed a variety of material strategies to "invade" public space, or blur the boundaries between public and private, in ways conducive to expanding women's presence and influence. Institutions dedicated to domestic reform—various women's clubs, cooperative homes, YWCAs, and other voluntary organizations—were made visually dominant parts of the landscape. In some instances, they were purposely built as the tallest or largest building in the neighborhood. Domestic reformers also played a central role in the emerging City Beautiful movement. Women physically shaped and exercised control over public landscapes by introducing playgrounds, children's gardens, and green spaces.

Similar "little tactics of the habitat" (Foucault 1980: 149) were applied by reformers at smaller scales. Reform activists in Boston sought to move women out of poverty by experimenting with communal built spaces and socialized housekeeping in new cooperative women's homes. Archaeological excavations at the Magdalen Society Asylum in Philadelphia indicate that mid-nineteenth-century reformers used plain and edged white ceramics with the intention of instilling in their "fallen" women residents the moral values of modesty, frugality, simplicity, and conservativism (Spencer-Wood 1994: 194). More draconian measures such as massive brick walls were used to separate and protect the Magdalens from worldly temptations and other undesirable elements. But reformers were not always so heavy-handed. Archaeological evidence also shows that the Magdalen Society reformers loosened up over time, as evidenced by an increase in decorated ceramics in asylum assemblages and evidence for the relaxing of other rules. Reformers were also capable of yielding to reformees who themselves exercised collective agency; witness the successful lobbying of working-class women to enhance their personal privacy through the creation of more single rooms at the Chicago YWCA (Spencer-Wood 1994: 195). Spencer-Wood's work clearly shows the archaeological potential of domestic reform sites to inform about women's collective agency and the negotiations between reformers and working-class women over how to construct women-friendly built environments.

Diana Wall's (1999; also 1991, 1994) work in New York City also focuses on the dynamics of gender, class, and materiality. Her study of ceramic assemblages of working- and middle-class households in nineteenth-century Greenwich Village illuminates class-based differences in consumer patterns in ways that disclose female collective agency (Wall 1999). Wall interprets middle- and upper-class use of Gothic twelve-sided ironstone plates as related to the perceived role of women as guardians of a family's and society's morals. An Italianate style that paralleled the genteel style of middle-class architecture is interpreted in the same way; the style created good moral character and good people. In contrast, working-class households used a whole array of molded designs absent from middle- and upper-class assemblages. While the meaning of this variation is not entirely clear, working-class people were certainly not emulating middle and upper classes' understandings of women as moral guardians of the home.

Wall (1991) also compared the teaware from a working-class family to the teaware from a middle-class family. Both households had plain, paneled Gothic wares that were similar to the tableware. The two households differed in that the middle-class family had a second set of decorated porcelain teaware. Wall associates the two kinds of teaware with use in different social settings: morning and afternoon tea. Morning tea was a family affair, while afternoon tea was a venue for socializing with community members. She suggests that middle-class women had a greater investment in displaying their status as way to impress upon friends the refinement and gentility of their families and to elevate their family's position in the class structure. Lower-class women lacked this interest. Instead, sharing tea may have been a way to create and affirm cooperative social relations. Rather than asserting their status through decorated porcelain teaware, working-class women created community by using plain wares that did not elicit competition (Wall 1991: 79).

Finally, Amy Young's (2003) analyses of antebellum plantation landscapes show how African-American women and men used different strategies to provide for their families and build community solidarity. Women at Locust Grove plantation near Louisville, Kentucky, worked the spaces between slave houses and the communal yard between rows of houses. They conducted generalized reciprocal exchanges of items such as decorated ceramics, glass tableware, buttons, and other objects. Archaeological recovery of matched ceramic items and other artifacts from different houses indicate that these were shared or given as gifts among the slave families. These reciprocal relations established bonds of kinship that helped the community cope with the predations and deprivations of slavery. They ensured the future of children whose parents were sold away, provided emotional support during periods of sickness and solace upon the death of a family member, and reached out to new slaves entering the community.

Young (2003) also considered male roles at Saragossa Plantation in Adams County, Mississippi, just outside Natchez (see also Young, Tuma, and Jenkins 2001). Here, ethnographic, historic, and archaeological evidence converge to indicate the strategic importance of male hunting in slave communities. At Saragossa, males worked the fields, forests, and streams beyond the slave quarters and the communal yard. Male hunting of small game (squirrel, raccoon, rabbit) and some deer provided sustenance for the community. This was likely accomplished through clandestine night hunting, as predicted by Paynter and McGuire (1991). But the hunting also had social and psychological purposes. It served to integrate newcomers into the slave community under conditions of a constantly fluctuating population. And it reinforced male self-worth (that is, male as breadwinner) in a deeply emasculating slave system. Together, these different female and male activities strengthened the entire slave community.

Class

Several important studies have shown how workers struggle with industrial capitalists over the conditions under which their labor is appropriated and compensated and its products distributed. Paynter and McGuire (1991) is a key source for much interpretive theory in this area. They note how collective resistance by workers in an industrial setting can take many forms, including malingering, sabotage of machinery, and destruction of products—strategies that can all have archaeological correlates.

Nassaney and Abel (1993, 2000) investigated such strategies in the Connecticut River valley of western Massachusetts. They analyzed material remains at the John Russell Cutlery Company in Turner's Falls, one of the world's leading nineteenth-century knife manufacturers. Relocated from Greenfield and opened in 1870, the Turner's Falls plant was a prototype modern cutlery factory. Major modernization in the 1880s was informed by new techniques of managing work that separated product conception and production, subdivided the process of production, and standardized production tasks. These techniques degraded human labor by de-skilling the work force (Braverman 1974). Archaeologists found a large quantity of artifacts related to primary production along the factory's riverbank. Discarded materials included inferior and imperfect manufactured parts from various stages of the production process. Nassaney and Abel interpret this material as the residue of worker contempt toward, and defiance of, the new system of closely regulated work discipline. Workers may have intentionally spoiled knives—a kind of industrial sabotage—as a way to assert some degree of autonomy on the shop floor. Documentary evidence suggests that the historical context was exactly right for expecting such action. Declining real wages, deteriorating work conditions, and layoffs produced frequent disputes between managers and workers in the late nineteenth century.

Shackel (2000, 2004) offers similar sorts of insights in his study of nineteenth-century sites in Harpers Ferry, West Virginia. Here, renovation of the local beer bottling works revealed hundreds of bottles accumulated in the factory walls and in the basement of the building's elevator shaft. All bottles date between 1893 and 1909. Working conditions at this time were deplorable: workers suffered fourteen-hour days and exposure to dramatic temperature swings and noxious acids. Accident rates were 30 percent higher than in other trades. Evidence from the walls and shaft suggests that workers intentionally and covertly consumed the products of their labor and concealed their subversive behavior by disposing of otherwise reusable bottles out of the view of their supervisors. These workers were, in effect, defying industrial discipline by drinking the owner's profits.

Shackel (2000) also compared household assemblages of managers and workers employed at the local armory during the mid-nineteenth-century transition from piecework to wage labor. Archaeological excavations revealed differences between managers and wage laborers in the consumption of tablewares. The houses of managers displayed the latest goods, including pearlwares, whitewares, and ceramics with shell and transfer print designs. Managers were thus fully embracing the consumer culture associated with industrialization. In contrast, houses of wage laborers contained unfashionable, out-of-date goods like creamwares and shell-edged ceramics. Shackel suggests that this working-class purchasing behavior was purposeful, motivated by a nostalgic longing for the "good old days" when family members had more control over their everyday lives. The assemblages recall a time when husbands were craftsmen and when wives had better access to markets. Working-class men and women thus exercised agency in a way that critiqued the new industrial system.

Finally, the work of Beaudry, Cook, and Mrozowski (1991; Beaudry and Mrozowski 2001) at Boott Mills in Lowell, Massachusetts, explores how nineteenth- and twentieth-century workers expressed class identity and personal aspirations in a tightly managed environment. Lowell was the nation's first mass industrial city, and corporate paternalism loomed large. Lowell is the archetypal example of town planning for social control, and it provided a model that was emulated elsewhere. Industrialists in Lowell incorporated landscape as an active element in the reinforcement of social class distinctions. They located the textile mill, worker housing, and manager housing close together as a way to maximize surveillance and control and also to accentuate hierarchical structure. The construction of standardized worker housing with rooms of uniform size would have sent a message of worker expendability and interchangeability, thereby producing compliance with the status quo. In contrast, manager houses were distinguished by higher-quality facing materials and more fashionable interiors (Mrozowski 1991).

Excavations in the back lots of typical boardinghouses, however, produced abundant evidence of worker noncompliance with the strict social order. Despite their limited power and economic means, workers were apparently creating their own identities and building up a subculture of resistance. An abundance of medicine bottles suggests consumption for alcohol content, as a way to defy the company's discouraging of drinking and other efforts to control workers' leisure. Workers also created a particular category of objects—short-stemmed white clay pipes—to express membership, and pride, in the working class. But workers were not entirely rejecting the notion of upward class mobility. Aspirations in this direction are indicated by ceramics suggesting middle-class dining habits and inexpensive costume jewelry that imitates costlier class-conscious items.

Elite Collective Action: The Archaeology of Perpetrators

This chapter has focused on archaeological studies that enrich our understanding of collective action by politically dominated and economically marginalized groups. But as noted earlier, we also need what Pollack and Bernbeck (forthcoming) bluntly describe as an "archaeology of perpetrators." For Pollack and Bernbeck, too much focus on resistance risks masking the abusive power of dominant groups. They argue that we must expose the action of those who contributed to oppression through the raw application of power and, I would argue, through more subtle ideological efforts to create subjectivities that would serve elite class interests.

Leone's work on eighteenth-century Annapolis sites and material cultures, briefly discussed in chapter 3, gives us insight into how elite perpetrators worked in both overt and subtle ways. As noted there, Leone's work has invited criticism as unjustifiably reinforcing the "dominant ideology" thesis that portrays nonelites as passive consumers of ideas that work against their better interests. We can debate how much of this manipulation was premeditated by colonial elites planning and acting in concert, though it is notable that many of the elites in question were cosignatories of the Declaration of Independence.

Minimally, Leone and other Annapolis researchers give us some substantial traction for producing an archaeology of perpetrators.

The rich literature on corporate town planning provides other indicators of how elites structure the material world in ways that maximize capitalist exploitation and surplus accumulation. We have already noted the Lowell model of corporate-controlled landscape and building design. Shackel (2004) reviews some other studies of perpetrators in an industrial capitalist context. At Virginus Island, near Harpers Ferry, Abraham Herr sought to do what the paternalistic industrialists at Lowell did: he standardized the workers' built environment, plus he employed panoptic (Foucault 1979) principles of worker surveillance by locating his house within close eyesight of worker housing and his mill. In work that touches on the Colorado coalfield case study presented below, Hardesty (1998) shows how hierarchy and power were encoded in the town plans, settlement pattern, and wider landscape of the mining West. The model company town of McGill in eastern Nevada straightforwardly reflects—and naturalizes—class stratification via use of a zonal model: high-ranking company officials were situated in "The Circle," middle managers in "middle town," and workers in "lower town." Other landmark studies show how such spatial differentiation and control were created at larger geographical scales, including the region and the world system (Paynter 1982).

Although Pollack and Bernbeck see an archaeology of perpetrators as a necessary counterweight to an identity-oriented archaeology, they admit that there is priority to studying those who have suffered from perpetrators' acts. Their proposal overlaps in other ways with the archaeology of collective action advocated here. Pollack and Bernbeck are explicit in saying that their principal goal is to provoke controversial public discourse, not to create a coherent narrative about the past. Of course, provoking debate and producing coherent, empirically informed narratives are both important processes in an explanatory and emancipatory archaeology.

Summary

Historical archaeologists have done yeoman's work to illuminate race-, gender-, and class-based forms of collective action. They have documented strategies that disenfranchised people in various political and economic circumstances use to cope with social inequality and oppression. These studies also illustrate archaeology's emancipatory power. What Orser (1998: 76) says about Mullins' work also goes for that of the others: it has "potential meaning for all people seeking to understand how the social inequalities of today were materially expressed in the past, even in fairly recent history." This work pierces the veil of legitimizing ideology that often informs the master narratives of official history. This is so much the better for pointing up how today's social inequalities might best be challenged and eliminated (Mullins 1999b: 186; Johnson 1999). In the next chapter, I turn to a more detailed case study of collective action in the past, one that has an especially significant contemporary political charge.

Class and Collective Action
on the Colorado Frontier

A Brief History

This chapter sets the stage for the extended case study of collective action—the Colorado coalfield strike and war of 1913–14—by presenting historical background to the event. As noted in chapter 1, the Colorado coalfield strike and the deaths of women and children at the Ludlow tent colony are part of the "hidden history" of the West. This was forcefully demonstrated by a 1997 survey of visitors to the Ludlow Massacre Memorial that we conducted in conjunction with our archaeological fieldwork. Nearly 60 percent of the visitors to Ludlow arrive expecting to find a monument to an Indian massacre—another Custer Battlefield, perhaps—or some other episode of the Indian wars. They rarely expect a monument to American labor wars. This is powerful testimony to public ignorance of the cultural and historical processes that shaped the American West. Indeed, when described to professional and public audiences, the story of the strike never fails to impress and often elicits audible gasps.

National Context of the Coalfield Strike

The Colorado coalfield strike took place over fifteen months between September 1913 and December 1914. It was one of the most violent strikes in American history. It resulted in an estimated seventy-four deaths and an unknown number of wounded. The defining events were the Ludlow Massacre of April 20, 1914, in which twenty-five people (including two women and eleven children) died during a Colorado state militia assault on Ludlow, and the subsequent Ten Days' War, in which armed strikers seized control of the mining district. Although the strike was eventually broken in December of that year, the events of the strike and, especially, the deaths of women and children outraged the American public. The resulting congressional inquiry forced some key reforms in management-labor relations and was a turning point in worker struggles for union recognition. Indeed, Ludlow was crucial for delivering many of the workplace rights that we enjoy today, including the right to safe working conditions and the right to collective bargaining.

Although especially dramatic, the hostilities at Ludlow were not unique for the times. They typified a period of industrial violence that defined the first two decades of the twentieth century. This period is generally—and paradoxically—known as the Progressive Era. During the Progressive Era, industrialization was established as the driving economic force in American society. Resources, human labor, and machine technology were brought together in largely urban contexts of factory production. Industrial production was accompanied by a deepening social class division between those who owned the technological means of producing wealth and those who contributed labor for its production. Progressive Era violence was thus sparked by two conflicting, class-based visions of workplace relations. Capital's vision privileged ownership as the most important party, on the assumption that entrepreneurs take all the risks in producing national wealth. Labor's vision saw workers as central, given that worker effort directly creates national wealth.

Progressive Era clashes between capital and labor were as intense in the United States as in any other nation faced with rapid economic and political change. Strikes, riots, and massacres punctuated the late 1800s and early 1900s at regular intervals. On May 3, 1886, police killed four strikers and wounded many others during a violent confrontation between unionized workers and nonunion strikebreakers at the McCormick Reaper Works in Chicago. This incident preceded by one day the bombing in Haymarket Square that killed and wounded several police and protestors. On July 6, 1892, Pinkerton Security guards opened fire on striking Carnegie mill steelworkers in Homestead, Pennsylvania. Eleven strikers and spectators and seven guards were shot to death. On September 10, 1897, nineteen unarmed striking coal miners and mine workers were killed and thirty-six wounded by a sheriff's posse for refusing to disperse near Lattimer, Pennsylvania. On June 8, 1904, a battle between state militia and striking miners at Dunnville, Colorado, ended with six union members dead and fifteen taken prisoner. On December 25, 1909, a bomb destroyed a portion of the Llewellyn Ironworks in Los Angeles, where a bitter strike was in progress. On February 24, 1912, women and children were beaten by police during a textile strike in Lawrence, Massachusetts. Numerous other examples from across the nation could be cited.

Ludlow's distinctiveness in this context of industrial violence stemmed from its relative geographical isolation on the western frontier and its number of women and children casualties (McGovern and Guttridge 1972). It was also distinctive in terms of its especially high concentration of immigrant labor.

Immigration combined with industrialization to form a volatile context for Progressive Era conflict. Many immigrants to America came to establish new lives, but others were looking for income that they could use to improve their lives back in their home countries.

Whatever their motives, Progressive Era immigrant workers (like immigrants during earlier periods of industrialization) mostly came from rural, preindustrial backgrounds. They were new to industrial production, and thus they brought work habits to the factory gate that could frustrate discipline- and cost-conscious manufacturers (Gutman 1977). American work rules and the idea of the workweek also conflicted with a variety of other old country cultural and religious practices. Gutman (1977) provides a number of examples. A Polish wedding in a Pennsylvania mining or mill town lasted three to five days. Eastern European Orthodox Jews held a festival eight days after the birth of a son without regard to what particular day that was (Gutman 1977: 23). Greek and Roman Catholic workers shared the same jobs but observed different holy days, which was an annoyance to many employers. A recurrent tension thus existed between native-born and immigrant men and women fresh to the factory and the demands imposed on them by the regularities and disciplines of factory labor (Gutman 1977: 13).

Industrialization and immigration opened doors to intensified exploitation of working people by corporate interests all across the United States. There were no laws protecting workers' rights or union activity in 1913–14. Workers in many places were denied freedoms of speech and assembly. Although labor's cause to redress these conditions was not always a noble struggle for justice (Foote 1997), in almost every instance the fight between capital and labor was unequal. Capital was able to mobilize tremendous resources, from control of railroads and the telegraph to control of local police and government, to further its agenda and suppress labor's cause. Progressive Era political and economic discourse came to be dominated by, as framed by Gitelman (1988: xi), the labor question: "Can some way be found to accommodate the interests of Capital and Labor, or is their conflict—often violent and almost always incendiary in its emotional charge—bound to breach the existing order?"

The hostilities at Ludlow also exemplified processes and conflicts extending deeper into the history of the American West. The American West has long enjoyed romantic, mythic status as an open, empty region where rugged, bootstrapping individuals could make their fortunes unfettered by the constraints of class and ethnic background. The scholarly work of Frederick Jackson Turner, especially his 1893 essay "The Significance of the Frontier in

American History," did much to advance this triumphal narrative of western history (see also Turner 1920) that in many ways anchors the official histories of America described in chapter 3.

Though Turner's work was crucial for legitimizing the study of western history, it left much out of the story. New Western historians, among others, have gunned down the romantic Turnerian image (Limerick 1987, 1991; Cronon, Miles, and Gitlin 1992; see also Smith 1950; Nash 1991). They have demonstrated the embeddedness of western life and culture in larger historical processes of conquest, ethnic conflict, population migration, economic exploitation, and political domination. They have shown the effect of these processes on all sectors of societies and on a variety of ethnic groups.

Indeed, even the West's great iconic symbol of economic free agency and self-sufficiency—the cowboy—is now known to have been shaped by capitalist class relationships centered in the industrializing East. Many cowboys were wage laborers in the employ of ranches that were organized as joint stock companies. Many did not even own their own horses. As Papanikolas (1995: 75) puts it, "Strip a cowboy of his horse . . . [and he was] but one more seasonal worker attached to the industrial world by railroads that led to Chicago stockyards and ranches owned as often as not by Eastern bankers or Scottish investors." The freedom of the cowboy was simply the freedom to choose his own master (McGuire and Reckner 2002). Most Americans have heard about the 1881 gunfight at the OK Corral; many fewer have heard about the 1883 Texas cowboy strike in which several hundred cowboys walked off their jobs at five major ranches (Curtin 1991: 56–59) or the 1885 cowboy strike on Wyoming's Sweetwater (Papanikolas 1995; McGuire and Reckner 2002). Wallace Stegner, arguably our leading chronicler and writer about western life, noted, "Cowboys didn't make the West; they only created the image by which it is mis-known. People like Louis Tikas [the fiery Greek leader of the Ludlow tent colony] made the West . . . " (Stegner 1982: xviii).

Class struggle of the sort that would explode with particular ferocity at Ludlow is thus deeply embedded in the history of the West. Indeed, Ludlow is generally regarded as the best example of open class warfare in American history. In the words of George West, a federal investigator of the coalfield strike, "This rebellion constituted perhaps one of the nearest approaches to civil war and revolution ever known in this country in connection with an industrial conflict" (quoted in Long 1989a: 170). This is an astonishing fact for many Americans. Astonishing, because we Americans need our myths, especially myths of simpler, timeless places that can serve as an antidote to the economic uncertainty and political insecurity of modern times. New Western historians have connected belief in a West devoid of conflict and struggle to modern economic and political anxieties that require—for their containment—seamless, mythic, and triumphal narratives (Cronon, Miles, and Gitlin 1992).

History of the Colorado Coalfield Strike

Several excellent and widely known histories of the Colorado coalfield strike inform the following summary. These include Beshoar's *Out of the Depths* (1942), McGovern and Guttridge's *Great Coalfield War* (1972), Papanikolas's *Buried Unsung* (1982), and Long's *Where the Sun Never Shines* (1989a). Useful lesser-known sources include Caputo's *The Death of Spring* (1984) and Donachy's *A Rendezvous with Shame* (1989).

Prelude to a Strike

The southern Colorado coalfield is on the east side of the Rocky Mountains (map 5.1). It lies in two southeastern counties, Las Animas and Huerfano. The coal seams occur in the foothills of the Sangre de Cristo range. Coal mines were located up canyons where the coal seams were exposed by erosion. These fields were a major source of high-grade bituminous coal that was used to produce coking coal, or coke. Coking coal fueled the new industrial capitalism, especially the steel industry, which supplied rails for the expanding U.S. transportation network.

In 1913, Colorado was the eighth-largest coal-producing state in the United States (McGovern and Guttridge 1972). Because of the steel industry's need for a steady supply of coking coal, the southern field was heavily industrialized. It was also dominated by a few large-scale corporate operations. The largest of these operations was the Colorado Fuel and Iron Company (CF&I), based in Pueblo. Founded through an 1892 merger of the Colorado Fuel Company with the Colorado Coal and Iron Company, in that year CF&I produced 75 percent of Colorado's coal. It became the largest coal mining, iron ore mining, and steel manufacturing enterprise in the West, earning the moniker "Pittsburgh of the West." In 1903, CF&I was acquired by the Rockefeller corporate empire. In 1906, the *Engineering and Mining Journal* estimated that 10 percent of Colorado's population depended on CF&I for their livelihood (Whiteside 1990: 8–9). In 1913, CF&I employed about 14,000 miners.

The mine workforce was largely third-wave immigrant labor from southern and eastern Europe, including Sicilians, Tyroleans, Tuscans, Cretans, Macedonians, and others. In America these ethnic groups came to be lumped as "Italians" and "Greeks." Mexicans and African-Americans also contributed to the ethnic mix. These workers had been brought into Colorado as strikebreakers in 1903, replacing an earlier, second wave of immigrant miners from Ireland

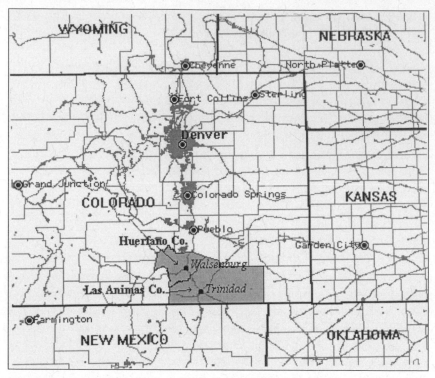

Map 5.1. Location of the southern Colorado coalfield.

and Wales (Beshoar 1942: 1; McGovern and Guttridge 1972: 50). In 1912, 61 percent of Colorado's coal miners were of non-western European origin (Whiteside 1990: 48). Before the 1913 strike, the United Mine Workers of America,
which sought to unionize these workers, counted twenty-four distinct languages in the southern field coal camps.

At this time, CF&I and the other large southern field operators had nearly
total control over the economic and political life of Las Animas and Huerfano
counties. Most of the miners lived in company towns. They rented company
houses, bought food and equipment at company stores, and bought alcohol at
company saloons. Many of these expenses were automatically deducted from
a miner's wages. Although it was made illegal by the Colorado legislature in
1899 (West 1915), scrip (a form of currency redeemable only at the company
store) was still in use in the southern Colorado coal towns in 1913. Company
store prices could be as much as 30 percent higher than those at independent
stores outside the coal towns (Long 1985). Doctors, priests, schoolteachers, and
law enforcement officers were all company employees. Entries to the towns

were gated and patrolled by armed mine guards (Beshoar 1942: 2; McGovern and Guttridge 1972: 23). Contemporary newspaper accounts described the situation as feudal (Seligman 1914a, 1914b).

As part of this coercive control, in 1901 CF&I created a Sociology Department charged with Americanizing the immigrant population by replacing their customs and language with American culture. CF&I officials—such as R. W. Corwin, head of the Sociology Department—saw immigrants as less than fully civilized and believed that only through education could bad Old World habits be broken. This was fully in keeping with rampant Progressive Era racism. The Sociology Department's publication for CF&I employees, *Camp and Plant,* was the instrument of company indoctrination (McGovern and Guttridge 1972: 10). Published on a weekly basis between 1901 and 1905, *Camp and Plant* was explicitly used to promote corporate policy and ideology. Its contents included articles that defined proper hygiene, sanitation practices, and morality, along with birth announcements and news about lectures, dances, and other community activities (Jacobson 2006). Americanization in the home was expected to produce more discipline in the workplace. Company schools—such as the Corwin School built in 1902 at Berwind—celebrated American values including temperance, a strong work ethic, efficiency, frugality, and loyalty to the corporate community. Along with the distribution of *Camp and Plant,* the company selected the contents of libraries and censored movies, books, and magazines.

The Sociology Department also employed material strategies to produce Americanization. For example, after 1901 it implemented a drastic change in company policy regarding the form of worker housing. Until 1901, workers could construct their own housing. Miner vernacular housing was usually made with materials that were readily available and low cost, such as timber, unshaped local stones, corrugated metal sheeting, flattened tin cans, and mud. Workers also chose to situate themselves among others of similar ethnic background. Margaret Wood's (2001) analysis of company documents revealed that in 1901 50 percent of households shared ethnic affiliation with two neighbors and 33 percent with one neighbor; only 12 percent had no affiliation. Such proximity likely facilitated community bonding and collective action. Beginning in 1901, CF&I took over the design and construction of domestic space and limited ethnic groupings. In 1902, *Camp and Plant* criticized the vernacular housing of miners as unsafe, unsanitary, unkempt, and "wretchedly inferior" (Jacobson 2006: 142). It promoted an alternative aesthetic based on a common style. The company standardized worker housing and its associated architectural features. This took the form of small, unadorned concrete-block cottages arranged in neat rows. These policy changes affected the distribution of ethnic groups. By 1910, only 15 percent of households shared ethnic affiliation with two neighbors and 41 percent with one neighbor; 41 percent had no shared ethnicity with neighbors.

Corporate power and control over everyday life were materially signaled in other ways on company townscapes. In Berwind, the Corwin School and teachers' housing, along with the superintendent's house, were elevated on hills at the north end of the camp, where they loomed over the houses of workers. Berwind's two established churches, one Catholic and one Protestant, were both located in the center of the camp. The positioning of these churches near the mining administration buildings promoted a material link between the company and religious authority. The town jail, built in 1912, was located directly across from entrance Number 5 of the Berwind mine. It was the first structure seen by miners upon exiting the mine, and managers perhaps used it to make a material statement about the consequences of challenging corporate authority (Jacobson 2006). Like the industrial contexts described in chapter 4, panoptic power was clearly expressed in the Colorado coal camps.

These and other homefront conditions likely took a psychological toll on workers and may have played a significant role in causing miners to strike in 1913. Of course, exploitative conditions in the mine shafts were of primary importance. Colorado mines operated in flagrant violation of several state laws mandating safety inspections and fair compensation of miners. Safety regulations were on the books by 1883 and were reaffirmed and strengthened by the Colorado legislature in 1913 (Whiteside 1990: 58–59, 106–8). Legislation mandating an eight-hour workday was passed in 1905 (West 1915: 21–22). In 1913, a southern Colorado miner was paid not by the hour but by the amount of coal he mined. This translated into a wage of about $3.50 per day (McGovern and Guttridge 1972: 22). Although a state law had allowed miners to elect their own coal check-weighmen since 1897 (West 1915: 64), miners suspected, generally with good reason, that they were being cheated at the scales by the company bosses who weighed their coal.

The Colorado mines were also notoriously unsafe. They were among the most dangerous in the nation, second only to those of Utah. Miners died in Colorado at over twice the national average, a rate of 7.14 deaths per 1,000 employed miners annually (McGovern and Guttridge 1972: 66; see also Whiteside 1990: 74–75). Mine explosions claimed many lives in dramatic fashion, but most miners died of more mundane causes, such as rock falls and plunges down mine shafts. The high death rate was exacerbated by the company's policy of paying miners only for the coal they mined, not for so-called dead work, which included clearing away cave-ins, removing debris from along haulage ways, and shoring up the mine shafts to maximize safety.

Hand-picked coroner's juries absolved the coal companies of responsibility for mine deaths almost without exception. For example, from 1904 through 1914, the juries picked by the sheriff of Huerfano County, Jeff Farr, found the coal operators to blame in only one case out of ninety-five (Whiteside 1990: 22). Instead, victims were accused of negligence or carelessness (Yellen 1936). One of the great ironies of the 1913–14 strike is that workers were probably safer during the period when state militiamen were shooting at them than they would have been had they still been toiling in the mines.

The range of ethnicities present in the coalfield obviously had consequences for organizing the miners and maintaining unity during the strike. It is well documented in the papers of Lamont Bowers, CF&I board chairman and CEO, that the company would purposely mix nationalities in the shafts to discourage worker communication and solidarity (Long 1989b; Clyne 1999). The ethnic mix also resulted in the strike and its violence being seen—at least in the context of some official histories—as the result of a belligerent Greek and Balkan culture, rather than of the working conditions that existed in the southern Colorado coalfield.

The United Mine Workers of America was founded in 1890 and made its first appearance in the western states in 1900 with a strike in Gallup, New Mexico. In 1903, the UMWA led a strike in the southern Colorado coalfield. This strike failed, as operators successfully employed replacement labor and strikebreaking agencies (Vallejo 1998). This defeat did not extinguish the union spirit, however, and organizing continued in a variety of covert ways. In fact, Long (1989a) provides a strong basis for disputing the recent argument of Clyne (1999: 8–13) that the union in southern Colorado was "like a comet," streaking through and then flaming out with every episode of labor unrest. Union organizing—like tactics of resistance generally—often covers its tracks (Scott 1985; Paynter and McGuire 1991). Thus union activity likely had a more sustained history in the southern coalfield than Clyne allows. Clyne does, however, raise the interesting issue of the relationship between union organizing and the activities of the various Old World fraternal and ethnic organizations, or "lodges," that organized workers in the company towns (Clyne 1999: 75–76). These organizations may have collaborated with the union to foster worker solidarity during times of labor unrest. Their presence is clearly signaled in the archaeological deposits at Ludlow (chapter 6).

In 1912, the coal companies fired 1,200 southern miners on suspicion of union activity. In the summer of 1913, the UMWA, spearheaded by national organizers such as Frank Hayes and John Lawson, opened its biggest push yet in the south. On September 16, a special convention of UMWA District 15 met in Trinidad and drew up a list of seven demands:

1. Recognition of the United Mine Workers union as a bargaining agent.

2. A 10 percent increase in wages on coal tonnage rates.

3. An eight-hour workday for all laborers.

4. Payment for "dead work."

5. The right of miners to elect their own check-weighmen.

6. The right to trade in any store, to choose their own boarding places, and to choose their own doctors.

7. Enforcement of Colorado mining laws and abolition of the company guard system.

The coal companies, led by CF&I, agreed to all of these demands except recognition of the mine workers' union. In late September, the UMWA announced a strike. Although less than 10 percent of CF&I workers were union members, approximately 90 percent of the workforce struck. This amounted to over 10,000 miners and family members. Workers who lived in the company towns were evicted, and on September 23, 1913, they hauled their possessions out of the canyons through freezing rain and snow to about a dozen tent sites rented in advance by the UMWA. The tent colonies were placed at strategic locations at the entrances to canyons to intercept strikebreakers (map 5.2). Ludlow, with about two hundred tents holding 1,200 people, was the largest of the colonies and also served as strike headquarters for Las Animas County (figure 5.1). The UMWA supplied tents and ovens recycled from other strikes and provided the strikers with food, medical attention, and weekly strike relief. This amounted to $3.00 per week for each miner, $1.00 for each wife, and $.50 for each child. Many important personages in American labor history became involved in the strike on the side of labor, including Mary "Mother" Jones, John Reed, and Upton Sinclair.

Confrontation, Conflict, Massacre

The coal operators reacted quickly to the strike. Replacement miners were imported from across the country and abroad. Baldwin-Felts detectives—specialists in breaking coal strikes—were brought in from West Virginia. Violence characterized the strike from the very beginning, with both sides committing shootings and murders (Beshoar 1942; McGovern and Guttridge 1972; Papanikolas 1982). The first casualty actually occurred in advance of the strike

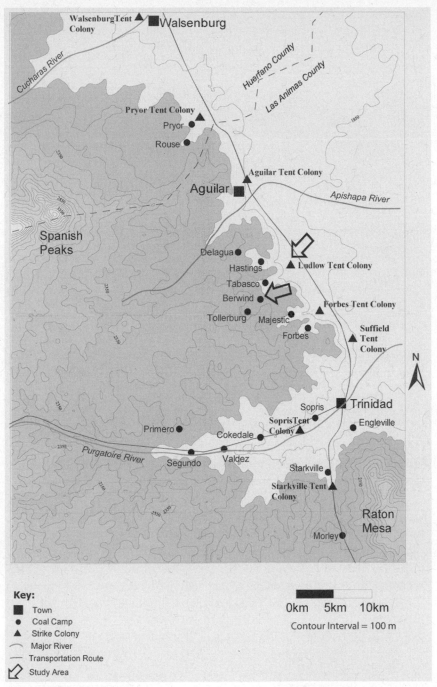

Key:
■ Town
● Coal Camp
▲ Strike Colony
〜 Major River
— Transportation Route
⬦ Study Area

0km   5km   10km
Contour Interval = 100 m

Map 5.2. Coalfield strike zone.

Figure 5.1. Ludlow tent colony before the fire. Denver Public Library, Western History Collection, Z-193. By permission of Denver Public Library.

on August 13, when a young Italian-American union organizer named Gerald Lippiatt was shot dead on the streets of Trinidad by a Baldwin-Felts detective (Long 1989b).

The coal companies soon mounted a campaign of systematic harassment against the strikers. This harassment took the form of high-powered search-lights that played on the tent colonies at night, surveillance from strategically placed machine gun nests, and use of the "Death Special," an improvised armored car that periodically sprayed the colonies with machine-gun fire. The first exchange of gunfire occurred at Ludlow on October 7 (Long 1989a). On October 17, the armored car fired into the Forbes tent colony, about five miles south of Ludlow, killing one person and crippling an eighteen-year-old boy. On October 24, mine guards fired into a group of strikers in Walsenburg, kill-ing four of them (Foner 1980; Vallejo 1998). The purpose of this harassment may have been to goad the strikers into violent action, which would provide a pretext for the Colorado governor to call out the state militia. This would shift financial burden for breaking the strike from the coal companies to the state. With violence escalating and the operators pressing him, Colorado governor Elias Ammons called out the militia on October 28, 1913.

In November, Governor Ammons issued an order allowing militiamen to escort strikebreakers into the coal towns. This indicated to the strikers that state power had joined the side of the operators (Long 1985). During the strike, CF&I billeted militiamen on company property, furnished them with supplies from the company store, and advanced them pay (Adams 1966). On a visit to the strike zone, Colorado state senator Helen Ring Robinson observed militiamen entering the offices of CF&I to receive paychecks (Long 1989a: 290).

The sympathies of the militia leadership exacerbated the tensions. The militia commander, a Denver ophthalmologist named John Chase, had been involved in suppressing a 1904 miner's strike at Cripple Creek (Jameson 1998). Following the pattern set at Cripple Creek, Chase essentially declared martial law in the strike zone. This period of unofficial and illegal martial law included mass jailing of strikers, the suspension of habeas corpus, the torture and beating of prisoners, and on January 22, 1914, a cavalry charge on a demonstration of miners' wives and children in downtown Trinidad. Women and children were important contributors to the miner's cause throughout the strike, specializing in the picketing of mine entrances and verbal abuse of militiamen (Long 1989a). In this instance, they were marching to demand the release of Mother Jones, who had been jailed earlier in the month for her organizing activities.

On March 11, the militia tore down tents at the Forbes colony. To one UMWA official, this indicated the beginning of a reign of terror designed to drive the miners back to work (Long 1989b). By spring 1914, as the cost of supporting a force of 695 enlisted men and 397 officers in the field gradually bankrupted the state, all but 200 of the militiamen were withdrawn. The mining companies replaced the militiamen with mine guards and private detectives under the command of militia officers. With this move, the neutrality of the militia was completely destroyed and it became little more than a strikebreaking force (Sunsieri 1972).

The exact sequence of events on April 20, 1914, is uncertain. As McGovern and Guttridge (1972: 344) point out, little has been written of the events that led to the Ludlow Massacre without emotion and distortion. The principals—coal operators, union leaders, militiamen, miners—have been cast in both noble and sinister lights. Much depends on preconceived notions about management and workers and the way in which one constructs, filters, and relates historical facts.

Rumors of an impending militia attack on the Ludlow tent colony had circulated for some days prior to April 20. The earlier militia attacks on Forbes and at Walsenburg provided a justification for striker paranoia (Yellen 1936: 234; Vallejo 1998: 96). At 9:00 a.m. on April 20, militia activity increased around a machine-gun nest on Water Tank Hill, located approximately 1.5 kilometers to the south of the Ludlow colony. Those miners who were armed took protected positions in a railway cut and allegedly prepared foxholes to draw machine-gun fire away from the colony. Rifle pits were also reportedly dug within the tent colony, a claim that can be investigated archaeologically (chapter 6). The militia then detonated two bombs, perhaps as a signal to troops in other positions (Donachy 1989: 86). Within minutes, militiamen and miners were exchanging gunfire.

After a few hours of firing, one of the survivors noted that the Ludlow tents were so full of holes that they looked like lace (O'Neal 1971). In the colony there was pandemonium. Some colonists sought refuge in a large walk-in well, where they stood knee-deep in freezing water for the rest of the day. Others took refuge behind a steel railroad bridge at the northwest corner of the colony. Many people huddled in the cellars they had dug under their tents. The camp's leaders worked all day to get people to a dry creek bed north of the camp and from there to the home of a sympathetic rancher. Many colonists ultimately bivouacked in the Black Hills to the east of Ludlow.

In the early afternoon, an eleven-year-old boy named Frank Snyder came up out of his family's cellar and was shot dead. As the day wore on, the force facing the miners grew to almost two hundred militiamen and two machine guns. At dusk a train stopped in front of the militia's machine guns and blocked their line of fire. The train crew restarted the train in response to militia threats, but by then most of the people in the colony had fled. By 7:00, tents were in flames and militiamen were looting the colony.

Toward evening, the Greek leader of Ludlow tent colony, Louis Tikas, the union paymaster James Fyler, and a third striker were taken prisoner by the militia. They were summarily executed. Implicated in the murders was a militia lieutenant named Karl Linderfelt. Linderfelt was a professional soldier, Spanish-American War veteran, and former head of the mine guards for CF&I. He had also been present at Cripple Creek as a company guard. Linderfelt commanded Company B, which consisted entirely of mine guards and was the most despised of all militia units stationed in the southern coalfield (Papanikolas 1982).

During the battle, four women and eleven children took refuge in a cellar dug beneath a tent. All but two, Mary Petrucci and Alcarita Pedregone, suffocated when the tent above them was burned. The dead included Mary Petrucci's three children and Alcarita Pedregone's two children. This cellar became infamous as the Ludlow "Death Pit" (Reed 1955; McGovern and Guttridge 1972: 210–31; Papanikolas 1982: 207–37). It is now preserved in concrete at the Ludlow Massacre Memorial. The known fatalities at the end of the day comprised twenty-five people, including three militiamen, one uninvolved passerby, and twelve children. Three days later, the Red Cross was granted permission by the militia to recover bodies. Lewis Dold, a local photographer who moved

Figure 5.2. Ludlow tent colony after the fire. Denver Public Library, Western History Collection, Z-199. By permission of Denver Public Library.

throughout the strike zone photographing strikers and militiamen, made compelling images of the devastation (figure 5.2).

When news of Ludlow got out, the UMWA and the Colorado Federation of Labor issued a call to arms to all working people in Colorado (Beshoar 1942: 183–84). Armed miners went to war. For ten days they fought pitched battles with mine guards and militiamen along a forty-mile front between Trinidad and Walsenburg. In largely uncoordinated guerilla attacks, the strikers destroyed several company towns and mines and killed company employees. The fighting ended when a desperate Governor Ammons asked for federal intervention. President Woodrow Wilson complied and on April 30 sent federal troops to Trinidad to restore order. The army confiscated guns from both sides and closed gun shops and saloons. The army also had orders not to escort out-of-state strikebreakers into the coal towns. However, CF&I president Jesse Welborn later testified that strikebreakers came freely to Colorado from other states and were protected by the army as they took jobs in the coal towns (Long 1989a: 299).

After order was restored, the Ludlow tent colony was rebuilt in June 1914, and the strike dragged on for another six months. During this time, President Wilson sought to broker a settlement between the coal companies and strikers (Yellen 1936). His efforts were unsuccessful. The strike was eventually terminated by the UMWA on December 10, 1914. With strike funds depleted and new strikes called in other parts of the country, the UMWA could no longer support the Colorado action. Some strikers with families remained on UMWA strike relief until February 1915. Others with families were rehired by CF&I (Scamehorn 1992: 51). Many drifted out of the state, and still others joined the ranks of the unemployed.

Aftermath

After the strike, mass arrests were made of the miners. These totaled 408, with 332 miners indicted for murder, including John Lawson, the main strike leader. Court proceedings dragged on until 1920. All the cases were eventually quashed, with most never coming to trial. The State of Colorado court-martialed 10 militia officers and 12 enlisted men but found them innocent of wrongdoing. Central to the defense of the militiamen was the argument that they were forced to take action because of the aggressive nature of the miners. A board of officers appointed by Governor Ammons on April 25 to investigate the battle at Ludlow heard testimony from witnesses who insisted that strikers started the incident (Long 1989a). Neither strikers nor unionists were interviewed. In its report, the board applauded the restraint and heroism of the militia and decried the "barbarism" and "savagery" of the strikers. John D. Rockefeller Jr. lent his voice to the militia's defense by arguing that the "defenders of law and property" should not be blamed for the fatalities. Nonetheless, by the end of 1915, Colorado's militia had been thoroughly discredited (McGovern and Guttridge 1972). General Chase resisted efforts to dislodge him until he was forced to resign in 1916. After Ludlow there was reluctance across the nation to use state militias to intervene in labor disputes (Albright 1975).

Although the legal court proceedings went nowhere, it was a different story in the court of public opinion. The Ludlow Massacre electrified the nation. Demonstrations and rallies protesting the killing of women and children erupted in cities all across the country (Long 1989a: 296). Nearly every newspaper and magazine in America covered the story, with pro- and anti-company editorials existing side by side (Long 1989a: 308). The *New York Times* carried so much news that the index of articles for three months totaled six pages of small print (Long 1989a: 308). Even the *Wall Street Journal* observed that a "reign of terror" existed in southern Colorado (Long 1989a: 308). John D. Rockefeller Jr. was excoriated in the national press and demonized in the eyes of the American public by such prominent progressives as Upton Sinclair and John Reed. Grim cartoons ran in both the mainstream press and socialist publications. In *The Masses,* John Sloan's cover drawing showed a miner, dead child in his arms and dead wife and baby at his feet, returning gunfire at Lud-

Figure 5.3. *The Masses* cover, June 1914. Denver Public Library, Western History Collection, C-760.097. By permission of Denver Public Library.

low (figure 5.3). In *Harper's Weekly,* Rockefeller was portrayed as a vulturelike creature hovering over the ruins of Ludlow with a caption that read "Success" (Long 1989a: 306).

In early 1915, a spectacular series of hearings was held before the U.S. Commission on Industrial Relations. The commission was appointed by Woodrow Wilson to investigate the events in Colorado. It included representatives from business, labor, and the general public. The commission's work exposed Rockefeller's role as a leading strategist in dealing with the CF&I strike (Yellen 1936: 220; Foner 1980). The commission's 1,200-page final report argued for workers' right to organize, restrictions on the use of private detective agencies like Baldwin-Felts, and the need for state intervention in protecting worker rights. The commission influenced President Woodrow Wilson to champion congressional bills in 1915–16 that would ban child labor and reaffirm the eight-hour workday.

The widespread national reaction to Ludlow focused attention on living conditions in the Colorado coal towns and on workplace conditions throughout the United States (Adams 1966; Gitelman 1988). Rockefeller engaged labor relations expert W. L. Mackenzie King (who later became prime minister of Canada) to develop a plan for a series of reforms in the mines and company towns of southern Colorado. Known as the Colorado Industrial Plan, these reforms called for a worker grievance procedure, infrastructural improvements to company towns (for example, construction of paved roads, provision of waterlines, electricity, cement-lined privies, and recreational facilities such as YMCAs), enforcement of Colorado mining laws, and the election of worker representatives to serve with management on four standing committees concerned with working conditions, safety, sanitation, and recreation (Adams 1966; Gitelman 1988). The plan also forbade discrimination against workers suspected of having been union members in the past. However, it did not provide for recognition of the UMWA or agree to the principle of collective bargaining (Adams 1966).

The Colorado Industrial Plan effectively established a company union. Feeling that there was little alternative, Colorado miners accepted the plan. It became effective January 1, 1916 (Scamehorn 1992). But critics such as UMWA vice president Frank Hayes condemned the plan as "pure paternalism" and "benevolent feudalism" (Adams 1966: 172). Mother Jones declared the plan a "fraud" and a "hypocritical and dishonest pretense" (Adams 1966: 172). Still, the Colorado plan served as the model for many other company unions, which spread across the country. By 1920 company unions covered 1.5 million workers, or about 8 percent of America's workforce.

What direct, practical impacts the Colorado Industrial Plan had on the lives of miners and their families is unclear. Some scholars see such industrial-era reforms as little more than corporate welfare or an attempt to continue, in keeping with earlier precedent, to control immigrant workers by Americanizing them. The conventional wisdom is that the plan produced some real material gains for workers in the company towns (Roth 1992; Crawford 1995). We are putting this wisdom to archaeological test (chapter 6). Even if substantial in material form, the reforms were limited in social impact, as indicated by the fact that the southern coalfields continued to be embroiled in strikes throughout the 1920s. The memory of Ludlow was often invoked on these occasions, and the site itself was utilized as a mass-meeting ground. At a strike in 1921, the UMWA erected four tents on the site of Ludlow in symbolic defiance of an order by the Colorado Rangers—who were well aware of the site's significance—not to erect tent colonies (Pogliano 1921). The Industrial Workers of the World (IWW or "Wobblies") also legitimated a 1927 strike by holding a meeting at the site of Ludlow (Whiteside 1990: 129). In 1928 the Rocky Mountain Fuel Company, under the leadership of Josephine Roche, became the first company in southern Colorado to recognize the UMWA as the representative of their workers. Widespread union recognition in southern Colorado came only with New Deal legislation of the 1930s, especially the National Industrial Recovery Act and the Wagner Act.

Summary

This chapter has detailed the history of the Colorado coalfield strike as gleaned from original documents and historical syntheses. The Colorado strike was particularly brutal, even by the standards of the age of industrial violence (Adams 1966). Although it ended in defeat for the union, the strike marked a turning point in labor-management relations and the struggle for union recognition. It moved capital away from violent confrontation with labor to more negotiated settlements. Most of the conventional histories of the coalfield strike, in keeping with precedent, are top-down and perpetrator-focused. In the next chapter, I consider what archaeology is adding to our historical understanding of the strike—from the bottom up.

Archaeology of Collective Action
in the Colorado Coalfield

This chapter discusses what archaeological research in the southern Colorado coalfield is teaching us about early-twentieth-century working-class collective action on America's industrial frontier. Conventional accounts of the coalfield troubles—if they are addressed at all in broader histories of Colorado and the West—tend to focus on famous people, events, and the organizing activities of the UMWA (Papanikolas 1982 is something of an exception in this regard). Although there is a rich documentary and photographic record of the strike, we have only anecdotal information about the everyday lives and relationships of the ethnically diverse peoples that comprised the labor force and the strategies of collective action they employed to further labor's cause against capital.

Archaeology, of course, is the discipline best positioned to flesh out this side of the story. The scholarly goal of the Colorado Coalfield War Archaeological Project is to help produce a more complete and accurate account of industrial processes on the western frontier. Specific research questions around collective action include the following. To what extent did the shared domestic experience of women and children in the company towns reinforce the class solidarity built up among men in the mine shafts? Once on strike, how did families support themselves, especially given minimal strike relief? How was the considerable ethnic diversity of the tent colonies integrated to foster a collective class consciousness that could sustain the strike for fifteen months? To what extent did coal camp life really improve following the strike?

To answer these questions, my colleagues and I are taking a relational view of class (Wurst 1999, 2006). Class is understood as a fluid set of processes that govern the production and distribution of social surplus labor and that articulate in complex ways with nonclass processes governing flows of property, power, and meaning. Class relations are historically situated and complexly determined by kinship, gender, ethnicity, and ideology. We are interested in the specific strategies that workers used to resist exploitation, build solidarity across ethnic boundaries, make a living while out on strike, and interrelate with wider communities.

Figure 6.1. Ludlow Field today. Photograph by author.

We are also taking a comparative perspective on coal camp and tent colony life. The Ludlow excavations provide the strike context (figure 6.1), and we excavated in pre- and poststrike contexts at the Berwind coal camp about three miles above Ludlow (map 5.2), from which many of the Ludlow colonists came (figure 6.2). We are looking to evaluate official and vernacular (see chapter 2) accounts of life in the coal camps and tent colonies and to investigate other ways—unrecorded by history—in which miners might have been coping with their circumstances. Of particular interest at Berwind are conditions on the homefront that propelled the strike, since strikes are family affairs first agreed to in the kitchen before being reaffirmed in the union hall. We are also interested in evaluating the nature and scope of the material changes in coal camp life promised by the Colorado Industrial Plan.

The archaeological contexts at Berwind and Ludlow have good integrity and abundant remains. At Berwind we surveyed roughly 90 percent of the site but test-excavated only about 1 percent of it. We excavated about 5 percent of the Ludlow colony and shovel-tested about 60 percent. The Ludlow site is a Pompeii-like archaeological context: a snapshot of an occupied space destroyed suddenly by catastrophe, with little subsequent disturbance. The assemblages at Ludlow—clothing, jewelry, children's toys, bullets, cartridges—certainly speak to a hurried abandonment. The excavations occurred in twenty-three different areas, or loci (map 6.1). Loci were chosen using a combination of sur-

Figure 6.2. Berwind coal camp today. Photograph by author.

face observations, ground-penetrating radar and metal-detector survey, and historical photographs of the tent colony. Within these different loci, seven complete or partial tent outlines were excavated, the most significant being the tent at Locus 1. Four cellars were partially or fully excavated, including Features 71, 73, and 74 and Locus 19. An additional five cellars have been identified and tested with an auger probe. One privy—Feature 70—was fully excavated, and the midden near the arroyo (Locus 7) extensively tested. All excavated material and related databases are currently curated at the University of Denver. Analysis of the collections is still in progress, but early results provide a glimpse of how the Ludlow strikers were coping with their circumstances. They also provide an interesting counterpoint to aspects of the documentary record.

Archaeology at Ludlow

I discuss the archaeological materials by moving from larger to progressively smaller scales: from location and layout of the community down to the contents of individual features. At each scale, I illustrate how the material world reflected the existential realities of striking miners in 1914, as well as how it was actively used to create and shape reality in ways that served collective action.

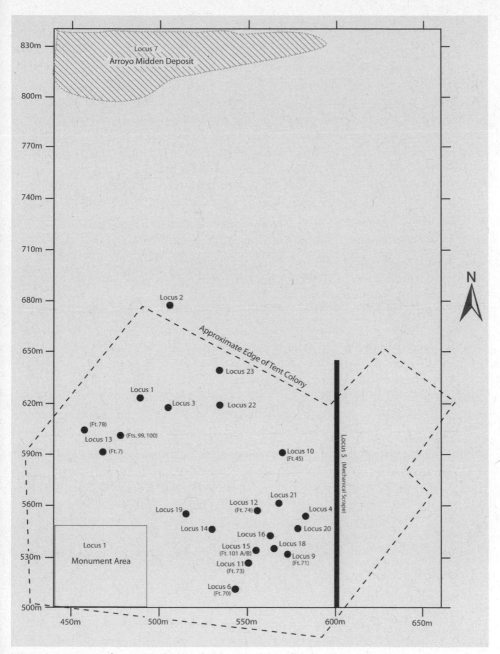

Map 6.1. Location of excavated units and features at Ludlow.

Community Location

Scholars investigating the materiality of class struggle often make a distinction between *space* and *place* (Williams 1989; Harvey 2000). Space is regional and global, while place is local. These strategic resources are differentially controlled by capital and labor. Prior to the development of the railroad and telegraph, capital and labor had roughly comparable abilities to command space. However, with the development of these technologies, the superior trading connections of capital gave it an edge. These technologies allowed capital to quickly move armed force to sites of working-class unrest and to spread information useful in eliminating other kinds of worker resistance.

Labor is much better at controlling place. Ties of kin and community link workers to family and friends employed in local business, health care, law enforcement, and other pursuits. For workers, such control has to be built up by negotiation between different place-specific demands, concerns, and aspirations and in ways immune to corruption by more powerful interests. Labor's control of place in southern Colorado was facilitated by tapping, in a variety of ways, the goodwill of local citizens.

Foremost was the goodwill of those who leased to the UMWA the land on which tent colonies were established. The Ludlow colony was established at the opening of Delagua Canyon. From this central location near the intersection of two county roads and a railroad line, colonists could monitor the movements of people—company guards, Colorado militiamen, strikebreakers—into and out of the canyon. The colony became, in a sense, a picket line (Margolis 1985: 77; Jacobson 2006). This concern with visibility is also apparent in the layout of the colony.

Community Layout

The layout of the Ludlow tent colony (5LA1829) appears to have been strategic (Jacobson 2002, 2006). When fieldwork began, we looked for tents and cellars along an east–west axis on the assumption that streets in the colony were laid out parallel to the adjacent section road. We had great difficulty locating any tent features on that assumption. A photo-overlay investigation using a technique pioneered by Prince (1988) and Deetz (1993) solved the problem. We mounted a transparency of a famous premassacre photograph of the colony (figure 5.1) on the ground glass of a camera similar to the one that was used to take the photograph. We relocated the point from which the photograph was taken—a water tower on the railroad track that ran by the west edge of the colony—and simulated its height using a hydraulic lift. From this position, we looked through the viewfinder and saw the image of the camp superimposed on the existing landscape. Using stable landscape features as a guide, we were able to locate over 25 percent of the colony's tents.

More significantly, however, the technique revealed that the tents were laid out at a 45-degree angle to the section road, running southwest–northeast. The key inference here is that this diagonal arrangement would have restricted a passerby's ability to peer into the colony, essentially terminating their view at the perimeter line of tents. Such concern for privacy is not surprising given the centralized location of the tent colony in a larger landscape and the fact that the tent colonies were always subject to search by the militia and other local authorities. The 45-degree angle is further confirmed by the distribution of artifacts and burned coal ("clinker") on the surface of the site, as ascertained by "dog leash" collections (map 6.2). That the "footprint" of this angled orientation is still detectable on the surface of the site ninety years later is impressive. This constitutes strong evidence supporting the strikers' concern to limit sight lines into the colony.

Surface artifact alignments indicate not only a protected place, but also a well-ordered place. This ordering would have been important for ideological reasons. The conflict of 1913–14 was contested as much in the arena of public opinion as in homes and mine shafts. Like other labor actions in history, it was a battle for the hearts and minds of third parties. Recall from the previous chapter the coal company's paternalistic attitude toward workers as a class of people in need of civilizing. The Colorado militia also used then-popular stereotypes of immigrants as barely human to suggest that chaos and anarchy reigned in the tent colonies. In the report on the Ludlow Massacre prepared by the Colorado militia for Governor Ammons, officers rationalized violence against the strikers by emphasizing the strikers' savagery. Militia major Patrick Hamrock portrayed the women and children as "no more than dogs, or they would not be striking and living in tents" (USCIR 1916: 6941). His statement played into a view of the strikers as acting on instinct rather than rational thought. The militia's view of violent and barbaric strikers was echoed in their description of events of April 20, 1914:

> In such a way does the savage blood-lust of this Southern European peasantry find expression. In this connection we find also that without exception where dying or wounded adversaries, whether soldiers or civilians, had fallen into the hands of these barbarians they were tortured or mutilated. It is shocking to think of our Colorado youth defending their state and exposed to practices of savagery unheard of save in the half-believed tales of the Sicilian Camorra. (Colorado Special Board of Officers 1915: 16–17)

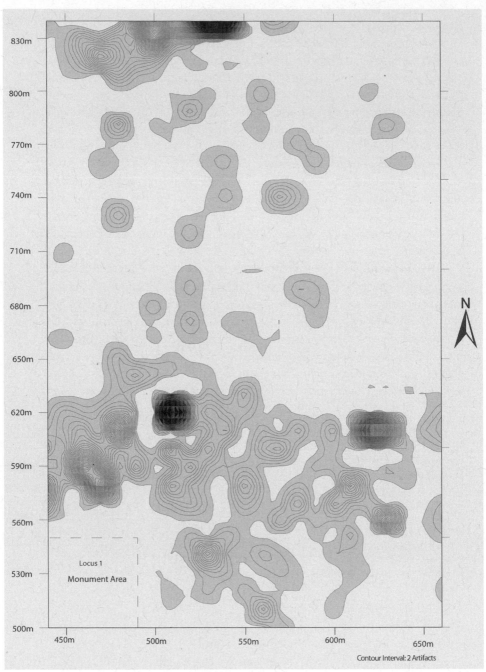

Map 6.2. Surface artifact densities at Ludlow.

Such views of the strikers as savages and murderers in turn produced expectations of the colonies as unplanned, disorganized places. Observers could see no central order; instead, they determined the layout of the tents to be completely random. Officers asserted that this created an unsanitary environment. General Chase stated that it was only the National Guard's "insistence" that the colony be vaccinated that prevented an outbreak of smallpox (Colorado Special Board of Officers 1915: 27).

Given this official opinion, the union was as much concerned to project an image of order and civility as to provide for defense. Documentary records (including oral histories, testimonies, reports, and photographs) substantiate the existence of material and social order. Mary Thomas O'Neal (1971: 108–9) described the colony's organization as a system of numbered tents on "numerically designated streets." Photographs of the colony show named streets—Front Street, Main Street, North Main Street, Second Street, Third Street, and so on—as well as numbers painted on the outside of tents. They indicate that Front Street was the street most open to the outside, thus suggesting that the union appreciated the public's perspective on the colony. Historic photographs also reveal that the colony doctor's tent was located on Front Street. This peripheral location was arguably less than optimal for serving daily needs. However, it could readily communicate to the outside world the community's concern for public health.

Thus, historic documentation and archaeological survey, taken together, confirm the existence of a rational, well-ordered settlement. The Ludlow tent colony went beyond the needs of shelter and defense to serve an ideological function. The orientation and organization of the colony not only promoted community solidarity but also sent a particular image of the strikers to the wider public.

Ethnic Organization of the Colony

A guiding question for the project is how the spatial distribution of ethnic groups in the tent colony compared with their spatial distribution in the company towns. As noted, ethnic patterning in Berwind was very strong at the turn of the century but was broken up by the company after 1901 as part of a strategy of Americanization.

Although the strike dispersed some ethnic groups (for example, Mexican miners, who had social networks outside of the camps), the same range of ethnicities found in the coal camps were likely represented in the strikers' colonies. The documentary record does not suggest that ethnic groups were differentially distributed within the tent colony. Instead, it indicates that there was a strong sense of integration and solidarity. Strikers established an internal police force and a group of committees representing each nationality. Louis Tikas represented the Greeks (USCIR 1916: 6364), Charlie Costa and Bernardo Verdi led the Italians (Margolis 2000: 35; USCIR 1916: 6808), and Mike Livoda helped organize the Slavs (Margolis n.d.). Through such a system, the union structured the relations between ethnic groups with the union remaining the central authority.

Mary Petrucci testified that the residents of the colony had good relations with each other. She made no mention of any ethnic disharmony (USCIR 1916: 8192). Helen Ring Robinson's testimony before the Commission on Industrial Relations is also pertinent in this regard. Recalling her visit to the Ludlow tent colony, Robinson found that "this long winter had brought the nationalities together in a rather remarkable way. I found a friendliness among women of all nationalities—22 at least. I saw the true melting pot at Ludlow" (quoted in Long 1989a: 290). Margaret Dominiske noted in her description of the colony that people expressed ethnic identity through music and that such expression was welcomed and encouraged (USCIR 1916: 7379). In the evenings, "Ludlow rang with folk songs—Italian, Spanish, American, and Greek" (Margolis 2000: 35). This is supported by photographs showing colonists playing instruments such as harmonicas and mandolins and participating in games such as bocce ball.

Baseball, however, was promoted by the UMWA as a way to bridge ethnic differences, a kind of Americanization in the service of collective solidarity (O'Neal 1971: 130). The strikers built a baseball field with viewing stands across the section road south of the colony (USCIR 1916: 6889). The striker Mike Livoda commented, "You see, they had baseball teams . . . and we'd go and have the best time. The miners all got along and no race barrier or nationality. It was just one big group that's all. And everybody just seemed to get along" (Margolis and McMahan 1975).

Traditional ethnic holidays such as Greek Easter were open to all strikers and their families, as a way to further cultivate solidarity. The women and children who took refuge on April 20 in what would later become the "Death Pit"—with the surnames Petrucci, Costa, Valdez, and Pedregone—were Italian and Hispanic and lived in neighboring tents. The only specially segregated group noted in the historical documents was the Greek bachelors (USCIR 1916: 6355).

What does the archaeological record say about the distribution of ethnic groups? As established by Wobst (1977) and others, personal items are particularly good in signaling ethnic identity. Many excavated artifacts reflect strong ethnic affiliations. There are buttons inscribed with Habsburg eagles, embossed bottles from Milan and the Adriatic city of Zara (Austro-Hungarian

Figure 6.3. Locus 1 tent platform, excavated. By permission of Mark Walker.

in 1914, Croatian today), and a variety of religious medallions. The fully excavated tent platform from Locus 1 on the northwestern side of the colony is associated with objects suggesting an Italian ethnicity (figure 6.3). These include
a crucifix and a suspender part bearing, in Italian, the inscription "Society of
Tyrolean Alpinists" (figure 6.4). A medicine bottle found in primary context
on the floor of a tent cellar at Feature 74 in the southern half of the colony was
embossed in Italian. There is direct evidence for a variety of other fraternal
organizations—Knights of Pythias, Knights of Columbus, Croatian Fraternal
Union—that provided solidarity and probably a hook for UMWA organizing,
as suggested by Clyne (1999). However, many other clothing items, specifically buttons, are similar throughout the site. They are made of Bakelite, shell,
copper, porcelain, and iron. There is not enough information from excavation
in any one area to substantiate the existence of ethnically distinct precincts.
Block excavation of larger areas is required to more completely explore this
possibility.

Thus, at the moment there is little to indicate the discrete spatial distribution of ethnicities within the Ludlow colony. The distribution of material items
suggests more uniformity than difference. Ethnicity was likely marked in a
number of ways, but evidence to date suggests that it was not something that
was explicitly used to segregate residents of the colony.

Figure 6.4. Religious medallions from the Ludlow tent colony. By permission of Mark Walker.

Tent Cellars

Family life at Ludlow centered on the tent. Some tents had cellars, which strikers referred to as "caves" (Pearl Jolly in USCIR 1916: 6348). The cellar under tent number 58, which came to be called the "Death Pit" after the Ludlow Massacre, likely typified many of the cellars in the colony (figure 6.5). According to Mary Petrucci, it originally had earthen stairs leading from the front of the tent to the base of the cellar, six feet below the surface (USCIR 1916: 8193–94). Strikers placed wooden timbers above the cellar, providing not only a floor for the tent but also a covering for the cellar.

Historic accounts of cellars suggest multiple uses. Most suggest that protection was primary, with the cellar serving as a place for occupants to seek refuge from the harassment of searchlights and the "Death's Special." Local informants interviewed by project staff along with accumulated folk knowledge suggest alternative functions as well, including a place to seek warmth during the winter.

Archaeological excavation of the four cellars at Ludlow disclosed that their volume varied from 10 to 20 cubic meters, respectively. The cellar at Feature 73 has proven to be the most informative about camp life, given its superb archaeological integrity (figure 6.6). The walls of this cellar are heavily oxidized from burning, and wooden planks lying in a parallel pattern suggest that they

Figure 6.5. Ludlow "Death Pit." Denver Public Library, Western History Collection, X-60482. By permission of Denver Public Library.

are the collapsed remains of a tent floor (Jacobson 2006). As discussed further below, these planks sealed material located in the cellar of the tent. The contents of this and other cellars confirm a variety of uses beyond protection from hostile forces and the elements, including storage and possibly habitation. Excavated cellars show signs of being very well prepared, with hard-packed and/or fabric-lined walls. One (Feature 74) contained a wall niche (185 centimeters long and 35 centimeters deep) that presumably was used for storage. As Jacobson (2006) notes, the strikers were experts in tunnel excavation methods, so we should not be surprised by cellars that display timber framing, stairs, and niches. The planning and organization evident in cellar design and construction—Jacobson (2006) describes some of them as bunkerlike—indicates that the striking miners at Ludlow used their control of place to dig in for the long haul.

Foodways

We are especially interested in what dietary remains at Ludlow can tell us about patterns of local interaction and support, specifically the extent to which strikers may have drawn on local merchants, ranchers, and other sources. Our trash pit, privy, and midden excavations reveal an enormous reliance on canned

Figure 6.6. Feature 73 tent cellar, showing collapsed tent floorboards. By permission of Mark Walker.

foods, much more than what we see in working-class contexts at Berwind. For example, the Feature 70 privy contained hundreds of tin cans including dozens of PET brand condensed milk cans (figure 6.7). Some of this canned food was undoubtedly supplied by the union. At the same time, other features contain lots of evidence for home canning, such as mason jars. This implies access to local farmers or gardens for fresh vegetables and fruit. Excavation of Feature 73 produced a large quantity of melted canning jars—certainly a product of the April 20 fire—located in the deepest level of the tent cellar.

It is interesting to consider the strikers' use of national brands in canned food and milk as a possible cover for local support in the form of prepared foods and garden and ranch products. As noted, the tent colonies were always subject to search, and thus any distinctive, locally produced goods might have been traceable to particular merchants. In his work on marginalized households in Annapolis, Mullins (1999b) shows that African-Americans purchased national name-brand, price-controlled foods as a way to avoid exploitation by local merchants. Strikers at Ludlow may have done the same but in this instance as a strategy to protect local, striker-friendly merchants from harassment by coal company operatives and state militiamen. This would make sense as part of labor's commitment to using place as a way to offset capital's greater command of space. Efforts to conceal locally acquired produce might

Figure 6.7. Feature 70 trash pit. Photograph by author.

also explain the stratigraphic location of home canning jars deep in the cellar of the Feature 73 tent.

Our most direct evidence of local connections lies in beer and whiskey bottles, whose embossing and labeling reflects Trinidad origins. The frequency of alcohol bottles is higher at Ludlow compared to what we see in the working-class precincts in Berwind. Work at other industrial context sites (for example, the back-lot assemblages at Lowell) indicates that social drinking is an important part of male working-class culture. Corporate control of the company towns meant control of leisure. Greater alcohol consumption at Ludlow reflects the greater freedom of workers from company surveillance given their control of place, efforts to relieve boredom and stress under strike conditions, or perhaps a little of both.

Faunal analysis—for species, cut, and method of butchering—is an important method for reconstructing community foodways. A total of 1,987 animal bone fragments were recovered and analyzed from the Ludlow excavations. The best-preserved and most-diagnostic material came from the tent cellars located at Features 73 and 74. A subtotal of 389 specimens (20 percent of the total) could be identified to species. Of this amount, over 25 percent was excavated from the single cellar at Feature 73. This cellar feature is thought to contain material culture that is representative of one household in its lower strata, with a jumbled collection of material from adjacent households located in the strata closest to the surface, a likely function of postmassacre cleanup.

The cellar at Feature 73 contained five species: cow, sheep or goat, chicken, pig, and spadefoot toad. The majority of remains come from cows, which might be predicted for a couple of reasons. Cow bones are relatively large and therefore are more likely to survive the elements of time and weathering better than smaller animal bones. But beef also lasts longer without refrigeration than other meat, so for preservation reasons alone, the colonists might have preferred beef. Two-thirds of the beef cuts were shanks from the fore- and hindquarters. Shanks are one of the most cost-effective cuts of meat because they provide more meat for the price than other cuts. This fact might also suggest provisioning from local ranchers.

Smaller animals such as chicken and rabbit were almost certainly consumed by colonists. However, the bones from these animals are fragile and not as likely to survive scavenging by animals and weathering. The Feature 73 cellar also contained the majority of sheep remains in the total faunal assemblage. The age of the two sheep excavated is approximately three months, and the bones lack butchering marks. We know from documentary sources (for example, Papanikolas 1982) that the Greeks in the colony celebrated Greek Orthodox Easter in 1914 by roasting a lamb for their neighbors. The sheep remains in Feature 73 could suggest that they are part of the population of young animals that were being raised on-site.

Butchering marks on animal bone can indicate whether meat was professionally butchered and sold by the cut or whether the animal was purchased in bulk sections and butchered by the consumer. The butchering marks on most of the faunal material from the site suggest the use of saws to process meat. Some of the bones from Feature 73 have chop marks from a cleaver or axe. All butchering marks suggest that an inexperienced person did the processing. This would make sense if meat was being purchased by the colonists, or donated to them, in bulk sections. More data are needed to sort this out, and broader excavations are required to investigate the extent to which meat was being shared across households within the tent colony.

Tableware and Teaware

As illustrated by Wall's work (discussed in chapter 4), tableware and teaware can provide useful insights into social relationships and agency within working-class communities. Gray (2005) has done a comprehensive analysis of the tableware and teaware from the Feature 73 cellar, which, as noted above, contains in its lower levels a single household's artifact assemblage, having good archaeological integrity. The assemblage at Feature 73 includes a full range of household items from furniture to personal goods. The number and variety of shoes and other personal items suggest occupancy by at least one adult man, one adult woman, and several children ranging in age from infant to preteen. Gray investigated the extent to which this immigrant family embraced the behaviors and material culture of Victorian gentility that anchored American middle-class values around the turn of the century, values that also penetrated the "Wild West" (Praetzellis and Praetzellis 2001). These values prescribed, among other material expressions, individualized, matched table settings and formal teawares. Though Gray's analysis of a single family's belongings cannot establish typical consumer behavior at the tent colony, it does provide a baseline for future analysis.

A total of 2,221 ceramic sherds formed the basis of Gray's analysis. They were sorted by ware, decoration, form, and refittable fragments. Minimum number of vessel counts were determined. The tableware assemblage contains an eclectic variety of vessel forms, including individual settings and serving vessels. The individual settings consist of plates and bowls. The plates subdivide into dinner plates and soup plates. The assemblage contains 27 plates and 2 clearly identifiable soup plates. At least 3 breakfast or bread plates were identified by rim diameter. The assemblage includes a matching set of 4 oyster bowls and 6 bowls of indeterminate size and style. The assemblage of serving vessels consists of bowls, platters, a pitcher, a baker, and a set of salt and pepper shakers. Nine platters and 8 serving bowls were identified. Three of the serving bowls are nappies, which are deep bowls of various diameters.

This assemblage led Gray to conclude that the tableware in Feature 73 is not consistent with genteel Victorian values, or what this frontier immigrant population likely took to be American middle-class values in the first decade of the twentieth century (Fitts 2002: 8). The predominance of plates with correspondingly few bowls is not in keeping with the segmented dining and individualized dining practices characteristic of the era. The complete absence of other vessels that would be consistent with Victorian dining etiquette, such as individual bone or butter dishes (Jasper 1996), supports this conclusion.

Instead, Gray suggests that the number of platters and serving bowls from Feature 73 indicates that in this household, prepared foods were served "family style," in keeping with the communal dining practices of southern and eastern Europeans, Latinos, and African-Americans (Deutsch 1986; Newdick and Rutherford 1997; Wilkie 2000). Gray used modern-day Tuscany (Newdick and Rutherford 1997) as a specific analogue. There, meals are communal events. Plates with deep centers and broad rims are preferred because they are versatile and can hold a variety of dishes from stews to salads. While Tuscans eat bread with every meal, they are more likely to place the bread on the table rather than a plate, preferring to use smaller plates for antipasti. Salads and pastas are served in large bowls from which diners help themselves. The large bowls are used not only for food service but also for preparing the meals. Small bowls are the perfect containers for olive oil, cheese, and condiments. Tuscan dishes are served straight from the oven to the table in the same vessels in which they were cooked. The tableware is often an eclectic collection of different styles of vessels. In short, the Tuscan dining experience is an informal event that emphasizes the communal experience of sharing food rather than formal dining etiquette (Newdick and Rutherford 1997: 8–14).

At the same time, however, decoration of the tableware from Feature 73 meets some of the criteria for genteel Victorian dining. While stylistic diversity is the norm, some of the vessels share design elements that have similar themes and constitute a near match. For example, three sets of vessels have similar delicate flowers in the same locations on each of the vessels. The differences between the floral designs are visually subtle. If value was placed on simply the presence of a floral pattern instead of a particular floral design, then some approximation of matching tableware would be achieved. Like the workers at Boott Mills (discussed in chapter 4), mining families living at Berwind and Ludlow may have expressed their aspirations for upward mobility by using ceramic styles that emulated middle-class dining etiquette.

The teaware from Feature 73 provides an additional glimpse into the social practices of this household. The teaware from Feature 73 is as eclectic as the tableware. And like the tableware, it indicates the maintenance of both traditional values and aspirations to American middle-class status. This complex balance is evidenced by the existence of two sets of vessels for serving tea. The first set is hand-painted Japanese porcelain and consists of a teapot and a creamer. This set has a floral design with gilded accents. This design is comparable to that evident on the tableware. The second set is whiteware with subtle embossing along the rim and base and includes a teapot and a sugar bowl. The assemblage also contains another sugar bowl that is green with white dots covering the surface. The final vessel is represented by one oval lid from a child's tea set.

The decorated, hand-painted teaware and the child's tea set suggest that the household was aware of the practice of using matched sets in genteel dining and recognized the importance of serving tea. Furthermore, the practice of serving tea was being taught to children, as evidenced by the presence of a miniature tea set. Moore (2007) points out that the remains of this tea set, and that of a porcelain doll also excavated from Feature 73, are very similar in their Victorian style to the children's toys excavated at other early twentieth century working-class sites. These sites include the property of Lucretia Perryman, an African-American midwife in Louisiana (Wilkie 2003) and a block of row houses in the Irish Dublin neighborhood of Paterson, New Jersey (Yamin 2002). Moore suggests that these formal Victorian similarities indicate that early twentieth century working-class children around the country played with toys that symbolized aspirations for upward social mobility. These objects helped teach proper modes of appearance and behavior, and served as material symbols of success for working-class parents.

But while the adult inhabitants of the Feature 73 household possessed the material culture that symbolized a Victorian tradition of taking tea, they did not necessarily fully embrace this tradition. A set of demitasse cups was also excavated from the cellar, suggesting that the occupants also consumed espresso or coffee. According to Mary Thomas O'Neal, a survivor of the massacre, she and her neighbors regularly shared coffee (O'Neal 1971). The occupants of the tent at Feature 73 thus may have sought to convey civility by using finely decorated vessels, but they did so on their own terms. They used their fine teawares to convey a message of gentility while maintaining their cultural preference for coffee. Through their daily practice, the occupants of the tent at Feature 73 negotiated a balance between traditional cultural values and those attached to American middle-class status.

As with the canning jars located deep in the cellar at Feature 73 whose stratigraphic context conceivably reflects conscious strategizing to protect outside sources of support, the stratigraphic context of the decorated and undecorated teaware in Feature 73 also might indicate conscious strategizing to build class solidarity. Most of the decorated vessels were recovered from below the charred floorboards in the feature fill, in the deepest part of the cellar. During the final excavation of the cellar, excavators noted that many of the vessels, including the Japanese teaware, were associated with metal hardware and wood fragments. This suggests that they were stored in a piece of furniture for safekeeping. The demitasse set was also excavated in this context. In contrast, most of the plainware was removed from the strata above the floorboards. This stratigraphic positioning suggests that the household used plainware most frequently in their daily practice, while reserving decorated vessels and the demitasse set for special occasions. These practices would parallel those reconstructed by Wall (1991) for her working-class families in Greenwich Village. In both social contexts, the use of plainware would not have elicited the sort of comparison and competition that could threaten community solidarity. That the Ludlow strikers chose to store their decorated and loosely matched teaware—as well as the demitasse set, an object perhaps most loaded with an ethnic "charge"—reflects both the value they placed on those objects and their commitment to building community solidarity.

In summary, Gray's analysis of table- and teaware from one cellar at Ludlow suggests that colonists were aware of genteel Victorian, American middle-class values that prescribed elaborate matched table settings and formal tewares. Yet in practice they incorporated only selected elements of that value system, ones that could conform with traditional values and, perhaps, a working-class consciousness. In short, they were not totally rejecting Americanizing influences but rather negotiating a careful balance between American and Old World identities that would serve the cause of collective action.

Archaeology at Berwind

The work at Berwind contributes to a small but growing database of archaeological investigations of company towns in the United States. Berwind is currently being developed as a residential housing project, which puts the archaeological remains at great risk. Our excavations—again, just about 1 percent of the total site area—focused on yards associated with worker housing. We excavated trash dumps and latrines in what we determined to be prestrike (1895–1914) and poststrike (1915–1931) contexts. The primary goals were to investigate economic conditions on the home front that shaped miners' decision to strike, and to evaluate the quality of improvements made in the mining camps as part of the Colorado Industrial Plan.

Archaeology identified a number of differences between the pre- and post-strike contexts at Berwind that address the impact of the Colorado Industrial Plan and its embedded ethos of modernization and Americanization. There were architectural differences between the two areas, with more substantial concrete foundations characterizing the poststrike context. Substantial differences in sanitation infrastructure were also apparent. The prestrike privies were earthen holes that were filled with trash when they became unusable, while the poststrike privies were concrete lined and, presumably, regularly pumped out. We also know that the coal company made a concerted effort to enforce prohibition after the strike. This is reflected by a relative paucity of liquor bottles in excavated poststrike assemblages at Berwind compared to the prestrike context and, of course, the assemblage at Ludlow.

Although archaeological research produced evidence that conforms to expectations based on what we know of the intended goals of the Colorado Industrial Plan, we need much more work to document the pervasiveness of reform improvements. Of greater interest are archaeological data documenting changing female strategies of household reproduction and evidence for certain forms of race-based identity maintenance.

Gender and Household Economic Strategies

Substantive insights into women's economic strategizing and changes over time at Berwind are provided by Wood (2002a), who coordinated much of the excavation at the site. Trash dating to before the strike contains lots of tin cans, large cooking pots, and big serving vessels. Mass-produced tin cans—especially large ones—comprise 52 percent of all metal vessels recovered. In contrast, food storage vessels such as home canning jars comprise only 1 percent of all metal artifacts. Households during this period are known to have routinely taken in single male miners as boarders to make ends meet, given the very low wages of miners. Census records indicate that at Berwind in 1910, 53 percent of all nuclear families had one or more unrelated persons boarding in their homes (Wood 2002a: 73). On average there were three boarders per household. Thus, archaeological evidence suggests that before the strike, women used store-bought canned foods to make stews and soups to feed the household. Wood calculates that through this activity, women accounted for about 25 percent of the household's total income. This activity also likely provided more variety in fruits and vegetables for the woman's own family.

After the strike, the coal company strongly discouraged—or, in Wood's (2002a: 77) words, "waged a quiet war on"—boarding as way to reduce worker opportunities for building collective solidarity. The company established and operated its own boardinghouses so that the behavior of single male miners could be more tightly controlled. Census records indicate that by 1920, the number of families taking in boarders had shrunk to 6 percent. Mining families no longer had income from boarders, and wages continued to remain very low. This forced some new strategizing by women on the home front. Excavation in poststrike contexts revealed significant differences in household artifact assemblages that reflect changed strategies. Big pots and cans decrease in the trash, and glass canning jars and lids increase. Mass-produced tin cans decrease to 38 percent of the total, while home canning jars increase to 29 percent. There is a significant increase—a doubling and tripling from pre-strike levels—of glass food preparation bottles, such as catsup, mustard, and pepper sauce. These numbers indicate that women were doing much more home food production after the strike to provide for their families. Poststrike deposits also show an increase in the bones of rabbits and chickens, as well as an increase in fencing wire. The latter likely reflects more gardening related to the home production of canned foods.

Wood's study of household deposits at Berwind shows how working-class women in the company towns contributed to the household economy in substantial ways. Moreover, Wood's analysis opens a window onto the shared existential realities and anxieties of women that were likely instrumental in creating interfamily ties of mutual support and assistance. These alliances would have paralleled those formed among men in the mine shafts. Both kinds of solidarity would have been required for organizing and sustaining the strike of 1913–14 (see also Long 1985).

Race-Based Identity Maintenance

At Berwind we also discovered some evidence relating to the theme of race-based collective action. Approximately 0.7 kilometers up School Canyon, a side branch of the main Berwind Canyon, we identified an area—described as Area T—consisting of a discrete cluster of domestic foundations, privies, and associated outbuildings (figure 6.8). When we first encountered these structures, we wondered why they were set apart from the rest of the community. Later, an informant told us that this was where African-American miners and their families lived. Preliminary analysis suggests that this neighborhood was probably constructed either just before or soon after the strike and was occupied until 1931, when Berwind was abandoned.

In Area T, we mapped a total of eighteen shaped stone foundations, seven privies, and five outbuildings oriented with the landscape on a high ridge overlooking the canyon. The archaeological remains are in particularly good

Figure 6.8. Area T at Berwind, looking east toward Ludlow. Photograph by author.

condition, presumably because looters or tourists have not impacted them. The foundations are constructed of substantial chunks of local stone that were roughly shaped into squares and rectangles. The stones are held together by a fine-grained mortar. The foundations are, for the most part, identical. They are rectangular, measuring approximately 8 by 10 meters, with internal subdivisions. The only significant difference between the foundations is that cement buttressing was used on the corners of seven of the structures. The remains of fence lines that once surrounded the houses are also present. The redundancy of design, construction materials, and construction techniques suggests that these houses were "company housing" and may have been built at the same time.

The most interesting feature of Area T, however, is the presence of a large, apparently communal oven at the western end of the domestic cluster (figure 6.9). This oven is unusual in that it is substantially larger than the other ovens at Berwind and is constructed primarily of local stone. Given the knowledge that African-Americans lived here, the oven recalls the collectivizing ethos that Ferguson (1992, 1999) and Young, Tuma, and Jenkins (2001) and others have documented for African-Americans living in the eastern United States during the slave period. We thus might be seeing in School Canyon evidence for broadly similar kinds of ethnic identity maintenance, if not glimpsing a subculture of resistance. Much more research is required to make this case,

Figure 6.9. Area T oven (unexcavated) at Berwind. Photograph by author.

assuming that inquiry into this issue—like inquiry into other questions still pending at Berwind—is not precluded by residential development of the modern landscape.

Battlefield Archaeology

Unaddressed thus far are questions about the battlefield logistics and tactics employed by the strikers on April 20 and during the subsequent Ten Days' War, that is, the form and dynamics of their response to, and open defiance of, state and corporate power. Achieving some understanding of these issues—as well as the logistics and tactics employed by the Colorado militia—is crucial given the expectations that draw visitors to Ludlow. It is also important given the long-standing controversy over the description of the Ludlow event as a "massacre." For some, this term is unnecessarily inflammatory and obscures the fact that killing went both ways (R. Walker 2005: 9).

Documentary and photographic evidence indicates that strikers were armed with Winchester rifles and shotguns and militiamen with Springfield service rifles and steel-jacketed bullets. Historians (McGovern and Guttridge 1972; Gitelman 1988) agree that strikers were heavily armed and that they stockpiled weapons and ammunition in cellars beneath their tents. They also suggest that strikers dug rifle pits or foxholes within and around the colony.

Our archaeological excavations at Ludlow confirm that strikers were armed with a variety of weapons including Winchester rifles and shotguns. However, the archaeological evidence for stockpiles of ammunition is ambiguous. Sixty-four percent of the ammunition recovered by excavation came from one feature, the Feature 73 cellar. This may verify that strikers did indeed have caches of ammunition and arms in the tent colony, but the evidence is localized and comparatively thin.

The alleged existence of rifle pits is more interesting and a more archaeologically tractable problem. Testimony from Colorado militiamen before the Commission on Industrial Relations and the militia's reports on the Ludlow Massacre repeatedly emphasize the existence of rifle pits within the colony. About Ludlow, militia lieutenant colonel Edward Boughton testified, "You must know, ladies and gentlemen, that in front of the colony on all sides were located carefully constructed earthworks and rifle pits, constructed in such a position as that any return of fire from them was drawn right into the colony" (USCIR 1916: 6367). Captain Van Cise supported Boughton in claiming that strikers used rifle pits around and inside the colony to trap soldiers entering the colony (USCIR 1916: 7328). Militia lieutenant Karl Linderfelt gave the most definitive testimony on the existence of rifle pits within the Ludlow colony. During the fighting of April 20, 1914, Linderfelt recalled, he entered the Ludlow colony in an attempt to save women and children trapped in tents and cellars but was fired upon by strikers occupying rifle pits (USCIR 1916: 6894). He also stated that the rifle pits for the most part were located on the southern and eastern sides of the colony (USCIR 1916: 6892).

Given such descriptions, rifle pits should have a strong presence in the archaeological record of the Ludlow colony. We should expect to find pits with no other use than as defensive structures, and their contents should be limited to arms and ammunition. However, thus far we have not clearly identified any features like those described by militia leaders. Feature 71, classified here as a tent cellar, is the only feature that could have served as a rifle pit. Identified through auger testing during the 1998 field season and excavated during the 1999 field season, its keyhole shape provides the closest approximation of a rifle pit. It measures 3 meters east–west and 1.5 meters north–south. It is smaller in overall dimensions than the excavated tent cellars of Features 73 and 74, but its orientation is similar, suggesting a tie-in with the overall layout of the colony. The artifact content of Feature 71, however, suggests something other than a rifle pit, including food remains, building materials such as nails, and clothing parts. Less than 1 percent of the feature's contents relates to firearms. Thus, the archaeological evidence suggests that strikers used this feature for domestic purposes rather than a defensive one.

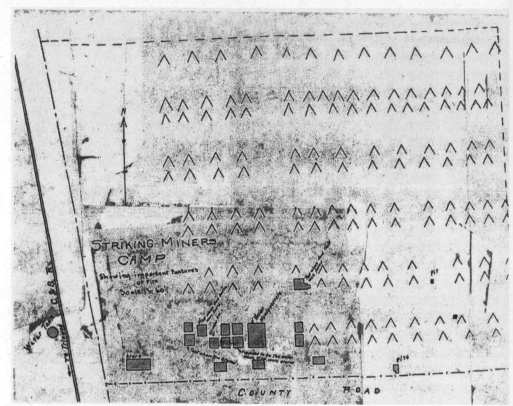

Map 6.3. Militia map of Ludlow colony showing location of rifle pits. Courtesy of the Bessemer Historical Society.

Another candidate for a rifle pit is Feature 70, identified here as a privy. Its location on the south side of the colony corresponds to Lieutenant Linderfelt's description of the placement of the rifle pits and to a National Guard map of the colony made after the massacre (map 6.3). But the feature has only three cartridges associated with it, and its depositional history is more indicative of a trash pit. If the feature was ever used as a defensive position, its use was likely expedient rather than planned.

We did find the majority of fired ammunition (12-gauge shotgun shells) in excavation units located along the western edge of the colony, in stratigraphic contexts that likely date to the day of the massacre. A person or small group of people may have been firing from this location on that day. This would make sense, since a walk-in well that historical accounts describe as a hiding place for women and children on April 20 was located just off the western edge of the colony. These spent cartridges could be the remains of covering fire to protect women and children fleeing to this and other safe havens, such as the railroad bridge underpass to the northwest of the colony.

Thus, there is no concrete evidence for the existence of rifle pits at the Ludlow tent colony. The absence of such evidence is also notable in that it dovetails with poststrike testimonies given by people other than militiamen. No other individual in the archival record describes or even suggests the existence of rifle pits at Ludlow. Thus, the Colorado militia appear to have perceived the Ludlow colony as being more dangerous than it actually was, or militia leaders may have purposely exaggerated the threat, and these exaggerations have been uncritically incorporated into official histories of the strike. Either possibility would fit with the militia's disparaging characterization of the colonists reported earlier in this chapter.

A systematic battlefield analysis that accounts for the actions of both sides in the conflict remains to be completed. Our ability to reconstruct battle tactics has been hamstrung by the reluctance of landowners to grant access to the militia camp located within eyeshot of Ludlow and to adjacent railroad cuts where there is a record of miners having taken up defensive positions on the day of the massacre. Further radar and metal-detector survey might help clarify tactical movements and positions. We also know that strikers sought refuge in the nearby Black Hills, located east of Ludlow, during the night of April 20. From there they may have staged attacks against coal towns during the following ten days of open warfare. Future survey in these and other surrounding hills will add to our understanding of miner troop movements and their coordination during the Ten Days' War.

Summary

Archaeological investigations at Ludlow and Berwind are producing interesting leads for fleshing out working-class agency in western coal camps and striker tent colonies. They are helping to clarify the day-to-day existential realities for miners in the shafts and families in the home. The work is making contributions that supplement, extend, and even correct the documentary record. But ours is still work in progress. We have much to do to substantiate the various kinds of material support that the besieged Ludlow colonists received from outside sources, as well as their novel, "home-grown" support strategies.

Future research on these and other questions related to battlefield tactics also promises contributions to general anthropological theories of warfare. Certainly we can contribute to what Otterbein (2003) calls "internal conflict theory" by identifying variation in the strategies used by contending groups to control space and place under conditions of internecine warfare. We can also contribute to more-holistic theories of warfare that bring together materialist and idealist or psychological motivations for conflict. Ember and Ember's (1992) model combining resource unpredictability and "socialization for fear" is relevant here. This model has been put to good use by Lekson (2002) in his study of post-Chacoan warfare in the ancient American Southwest. Both variables are relevant in the Colorado coalfields. Resource unpredictability produced the coalfield strike, and resource scarcity ended it. Fear of violent death underground, the explosive racism of early-twentieth-century America, and the "cultures of masculine violence" (Jameson 1998: 233) that shaped behavior on both sides of the capital-labor split created a volatile mix that certainly escalated hostilities. Both variables can be archaeologically tracked in the coalfields in ways that benefit general theory.

All of these theoretical efforts and ambitions accord with wider disciplinary concerns to illuminate individual and collective agency in the past. The methodological orientation and specific field methodologies also overlap with much contemporary archaeological practice. By producing knowledge about labor's history and significant contributions to national life, we add to archaeology's body of descriptive and explanatory knowledge (Hill 1999). In the next chapter I discuss dimensions of the project that connect to collective action in the present, in ways that further the goals of an emancipatory archaeology.

7

Archaeology, Public Memory, and Collective Action

Critical archaeology in the southern Colorado coalfield is adding to our knowledge of collective action in the context of American industrial conflict and is enriching our understanding of the American experience. Like the critical archaeologies discussed in chapter 4, it can be put to good use in the public sphere, in the emancipatory struggle for hearts and minds over the nature and meaning of history. This is the domain of *public memory*. Public memory is a body of beliefs and ideas about the past that helps a society understand its past, present, and future (Bodnar 1992: 15). Public memory legitimizes histories that are inevitably selective and partial. It silences and excludes alternative understandings, especially those that challenge the historical status quo. Understanding both what is remembered as public memory and why is important because public memory serves as tactical "power over" social settings (Shackel 2001).

At present, institutions of cultural production in southern Colorado privilege a particular set of memories that emphasize the area's place in romantic, mythic narratives of the Old West. The city of Trinidad celebrates its status as a rest stop on the Santa Fe Trail where wagon trains would pause to recoup before heading over Raton Pass into New Mexico. Rugged individualism, frontier conquest, and national progress are the dominant themes of this official history. It is a history of Kit Carson, Bat Masterson, and other assorted cowboys, sheriffs, and pioneers. It is a history that, through Hollywood mythologization, has attained considerable global appeal (Walker 2003: 74).

Histories of coal mining, company towns, and labor struggle—while not totally erased from this commemorative landscape—are decidedly marginal. The coal mining West is not the West that people want to see or hear about. When coal mining history is addressed in southeastern Colorado, it is sanitized and romanticized (for example, Clyne 1999; see also Lowenthal 1996; Karaim 1997; Brooke 1998; Poirier and Spude 1998). This is in keeping with observable trends in other deindustrializing regions of the United States, such as the coal mining and steel towns of Pennsylvania (Abrams 1994; Mondale 1994; Staub 1994; Brant 1996; Stewart 1997). These trends are disturbing because they do not serve the cause of accurate history. The central takeaway message from archaeology in the Colorado coalfields—like the message emanating from other crucibles of American industrial conflict—is that the taken-for-granted workplace rights and privileges that Americans enjoy today have a history, and a bloody one at that (for example, McGuire 2004; Saitta, Walker, and Reckner 2005). The marginalization and silencing of this history dishonors America and those who helped establish its promise of a better life for all.

Progress in commemorating aspects of a critical, countermythic history, however, is slowly being made in southern Colorado. In 1996 the homemade United Mine Worker signs on Interstate 25 directing people to the Ludlow Massacre Memorial were replaced by official Colorado Department of Transportation brown heritage signs. In May 1997, a memorial to coal miners who died in southern Colorado mines was erected by the Hispanic Chamber of Commerce in the middle of the Trinidad historic district (Bee 1997). The dedication ceremony was pro-union and relatively uncontroversial. This is in stark contrast to miner's memorials that were built—and then unceremoniously demolished—in other crucibles of industrial conflict such as Harlan County, Kentucky (Scott 1995) and Windber, Pennsylvania (Beik 1999).

At its inception, our project aimed to help explicate and better publicize southeastern Colorado's history of trade unionism and industrial struggle. We also intended, in keeping with the values of a critical social archaeology, to engage the local community in conversations about that history. Upon entering the field at Ludlow in the summer of 1997, however, we learned that the last mine in the area had closed in 1996. This led to a worry that our project would become little more than a postindustrial nostalgia trip. But these worries turned out to be unfounded. Archaeology at Ludlow has involved us more directly with industrial struggle and collective action in the present than we could have imagined. The rest of this chapter will tell that part of the story.

Ludlow as a Living Memorial

As noted in chapter 2, the Ludlow Massacre site is considered sacred ground for the descendant community of coal miners in Colorado and trade unionists everywhere. This community includes many direct descendants of people who participated in the strike. These descendants are primarily middle-class Anglos. They participated in the great social mobility of the 1950s and 1960s and are now scattered across the United States. Their memories of Ludlow are personal and familial. They are concerned that their family's involvement in history is remembered and properly honored. We have helped descendants locate graves of family members who died in the massacre, and they have helped us correct errors in archived historical documents and photographs.

Most members of Ludlow's descendant community, however, have no direct familial connection to the events of 1913–14. A small number of them are ethnic whites (Italians and Eastern Europeans), but the majority are Chicanos. They are the unionized working people of southern Colorado. Although the last unionized mine in the area closed in 1996, the descendant community is still actively involved in union struggles. Many of the everyday realities that provided context for the Ludlow Massacre—workplace danger, corporate greed, chronic tension between capital and labor—are still with us. Workers in a variety of industries in southern Colorado closely identify with, and draw inspiration from, the events at Ludlow. Since 1997 employees of Las Animas County and health care workers at Mt. San Rafael Hospital in Trinidad have unionized. Both groups chose the union of their fathers and uncles, the United Mine Workers of America.

Sometime after the end of the 1914 strike, the UMWA bought the forty acres containing the site of the Ludlow tent colony. A memorial was officially proposed for Ludlow at the 1916 UMWA convention by union president John P. White, and the proposal was quickly passed. Later that year, several hundred coal miners met at the site of Ludlow and joined the union. The Ludlow Massacre monument was officially dedicated on May 30, 1918 (figure 7.1). The

Figure 7.1. Ludlow Massacre monument, ca. 1918. Denver Public Library, Western History Collection, CHS-A847. By permission of Denver Public Library.

"Death Pit" under Tent #58 was also preserved as a concrete pit into which people can walk today. The monument is maintained by volunteers drawn from Ludlow's descendant community.

Because of the event's historical significance, the memory of the Ludlow Massacre is an integral element of working-class identity in southern Colorado. On the last Sunday of each June, unionists, labor activists, and sympathetic citizens from around the country converge on the site to remember the Ludlow dead. They have done so every year since 1918. The memorial service is a national event for the UMWA and serves as an opportunity to address contemporary issues facing organized labor. One of the more evocative artifacts recovered from our excavations attests to the site's long commemorative tradition. In an old privy feature, we found a bent and rusted wire floral wreath stand about 20 centimeters below the surface. The wreath was deposited after trash had been buried by silting and likely represents an artifact from an early memorial service.

Ludlow's use as a powerful political symbol in the great historical conflict between labor and capital was renewed at exactly the same time that we arrived to do fieldwork. Beginning in 1997, United Steelworkers Locals 2102 and 3267 in Pueblo, Colorado—about ninety miles north of Trinidad—began a strike against Rocky Mountain Steel Mills, the direct corporate descendant of CF&I. The memory of Ludlow resonated in that strike in that the steelworkers were fighting to stop forced overtime and thus trying to regain one of the basic rights for which the Ludlow strikers died: the eight-hour workday. The steelworkers made "Camp Ludlow" a powerful symbol in their struggle. They participated in the annual Ludlow memorial service every year and invoked the memory of Ludlow in other ways until the strike was successfully concluded in favor of labor in spring 2004 (figure 7.2). It took some time, but Ludlow's powerful symbolism eventually dawned on steel company management at its highest level. Faced with hard bargaining in contract negotiations, Joe Corvin, a former president of Rocky Mountain Steel Mills, complained that the steelworkers are "still mad about the Ludlow Massacre. We never thought about that. That culture is still there" (Strom 2000).

Other events on the national scene during the life of the project also underscored its contemporary relevance. On September 23, 2001, two explosions rocked the Blue Creek No. 5 underground mine in Brookwood, Alabama, the nation's deepest at 2,140 feet beneath the surface. Thirteen coal miners were killed in the explosions, twelve of whom had rushed into the mine to save a trapped coworker. Like Colorado eighty-five years ago, Alabama today has one of the highest mine accident rates of any state in the country. According to the federal Mine Safety and Health Administration, the coal company, Jim

Figure 7.2. Steelworkers marching at the Ludlow Memorial Service, June 1998. Photograph by author.

Walters Resources, Inc., has a mixed safety record. It counted serious injuries nearly double the industry average in 2000 (Firestone 2001).

The Quecreek mining accident that trapped nine miners in Pennsylvania in July 2002, although it ended with the joyful rescue of all nine, provoked additional questions about mine safety in America. Questioning has intensified with the January 2006 deaths of twelve miners from an explosion at the International Coal Group's Sago Mine in Tallmansville, West Virginia. The Sago Mine had received 270 safety citations between 2004 and 2006, many of them serious (*New York Times* 2006). In the three months preceding the explosion, the mine received dozens of safety citations and experienced three major cave-ins (Deutsch 2006). Mine operators knew of sixteen violations in 2005 but did not repair them until mine inspectors caught them (Urbina 2006). Sago is a nonunionized mine, and it is common knowledge that workers in such mines hesitate to report risky conditions for fear of losing their jobs. Three weeks after the Sago disaster, two miners died in a conveyor-belt fire at the Aracoma Coal Company's Alma Mine No. 1 in Melville, West Virginia. This mine had received 12 safety citations in the preceding six months for violations involving fire equipment, and additional reports of fire were ignored by supervisors (Urbina and Gately 2006). In May 2006, five miners died in an explosion at the Darby No. 1 mine in Holmes Mill, Kentucky.

Since 2000 the federal Mine Safety and Health Administration—especially the coal enforcement division—has been experiencing budget cuts and staff reductions (Roberts 2002; Urbina 2006). Yet events in Alabama, Pennsylvania, West Virginia, and Kentucky, combined with the coal industry's uneven safety record, suggest that enforcement would seem to be the one area that requires beefing up, not trimming down. Even without budget cuts, there are questions about MSHA's commitment to enforcing laws and regulations intended to secure mine safety and ensure the good health of miners. The outcome of the agency's court case against Jim Walters Resources is a case in point. On November 5, 2005, a federal judge vacated all eight citations and orders issued by MSHA against Jim Walters Resources for the Alabama accident, on the grounds that the agency did not prove violations ranging from roof control to mine dust levels to evacuation procedures. A total of $435,000 in fines was reduced to $3,000 despite dozens of complaints from workers about unsafe conditions in the Blue Creek mine. Like many other federal agencies in America today, MSHA is hamstrung not only by insufficient funding but also by staff incompetence associated with a "culture of cronyism" (Urbina 2006).

These recent mine deaths suggest that MSHA is seriously failing in its responsibility to coal miners in Alabama and elsewhere in America. As a response to lobbying by the United Mine Workers and other labor groups, an important step toward improving mine safety in America was taken in June 2006 with federal passage and signing into law of the MINER (Mine Improvement and New Emergency Response) Act. This is the first significant overhaul of federal mine safety regulations since the Federal Mine Safety and Health Act became law in 1977. The MINER Act calls for the modernization of safety practices and the development of enhanced communication technology for America's coal mines (U.S. Department of Labor 2006). At the same time, leadership of MSHA remains deeply contentious, with the UMWA opposing the current presidential nominee (Roberts 2006; UMWA 2006).

Thus, local and national events alike draw us into a contemporary discourse about Ludlow, the deep historical tension between capital and labor, and the relationship between past and present. The timeliness of the issues compelled us to use the project as a teaching tool (Walker and Saitta 2002) and to do everything possible to engage the local community. We scheduled fieldwork to coincide with the June memorial service, maintained an open site visitation policy, gave organized tours of the excavations, invited local citizens to participate as guest excavators, and provided on-demand lectures about our work to community organizations. We worked with the Colorado Endowment for the Humanities to offer summer teacher institutes that helped educators develop ways to incorporate Colorado's labor history into middle and high

Figure 7.3. Artifact display at the Ludlow Memorial Service, June 1998. Photograph by author.

school curricula. We were regularly invited to the podium at the June memorial service to update the project, just as Pueblo steelworkers were invited to update their strike news. On these occasions, we displayed artifacts from the original tent colony (figure 7.3) and gave numerous interviews to print and radio media. The *United Mine Workers Journal* publishes updates of our work to keep members informed. Such involvement continues to the present day.

The resonance of Ludlow in labor's struggle and, by extension, the relevance of our work were strengthened by a particularly dramatic event in May 2003. Sometime between the caretaker's rounds on May 7 and May 8, the granite Ludlow Massacre monument was vandalized by parties whose identities remain unknown. Two figures that anchor the monument—a miner and a woman cradling a child in her arms—were decapitated (figure 7.4). No arrests were ever made, despite a $5,000 reward for information.

At the annual memorial service on June 29, 2003, unionists in southern Colorado were out in force to rally around their desecrated monument. An estimated four hundred people constituted the largest turnout in recent memory. Various speakers put the significance of the monument in historical context and urged support for restoration. In a particularly stirring speech, United Mine Workers president Cecil Roberts described the Ludlow dead as American heroes and freedom fighters. He compared the Ludlow Memorial to the Vietnam Memorial, the Tomb of the Unknown Soldier, and the Lin-

Figure 7.4. Vandalized
Ludlow monument, 2003.
Photograph by author.

coln Memorial in that the Ludlow strikers died for basic workplace rights that most Americans enjoy—but take for granted—today. Representatives of several unions presented donations to aid in the memorial restoration effort.

While there is no direct evidence that the vandalism at Ludlow was antiunion, old-timers in the area say—in keeping with the character of vernacular history—that the vandalism "feels" antiunion. The visitor logbook at the memorial certainly records its share of antiunion sentiments. One entry equates unionism with socialism and communism; it expresses thanks that unions in the United States are "justifiably in decline." Suspicion of antiunion sentiment was also warranted given mixed public reaction to the Pueblo steelworkers strike. Some have speculated that replacement workers at the Pueblo plant committed the vandalism out of anger at strikers preparing to participate in the June 29 memorial service (Green 2004).

Even if the vandalism at Ludlow was not antiunion, it might as well have been, given the antiunion climate in America today (Saitta 2004). Political conditions are such that labor unions rightly fear for their future. Union protections are being denied to workers in several industries, pension funds are at risk of depletion through privatization, and as the recent flurry of mine accidents indicates, funding to ensure worker safety is minimal to nonexistent. Intolerance of, and hostility against, migrant workers is on the rise throughout American industry. But labor has been here before, and the Ludlow Massacre Memorial was undisturbed for eighty-five years before the vandalism in 2003, so the question of antiunion motivation remains open.

Media response to the vandalism at Ludlow also underscores the challenge facing advocates of critical history in America. The vandalism at Ludlow provoked universal outrage in union circles. It received widespread coverage on independent news Web sites and was the focus of a long article in the Mexican newspaper *La Cronica* (Delarbre 2003). Yet the national mainstream press outside of Colorado was resoundingly silent. This is notable if only because of the enormous amount of national media attention that the events at Ludlow garnered in 1914 (chapter 5). Plus, vandalism at public memorials is generally newsworthy material. Even though labor memorials are fewer, farther between, and much more modest than other kinds of memorials, we know from scholarly and informal channels that they take their share of hits. The United Auto Workers memorial to Flint, Michigan, strikers has been a frequent target for vandalism. A plaque dedicated to prolabor martyrs at the site of the 1886 Haymarket bombing in Chicago has been damaged multiple times by vandals. There is a tradition of coal miner memorials being dismantled not by vandals but by civic authorities in Harlan County, Kentucky, and Windber, Pennsylvania (see, for example, Beik 1999).

Given this, it is not unreasonable to expect some proportionality in the reporting of incidents. However, this is not the case, as revealed by recent research on public monument vandalism using several online databases (Saitta, Walker, and Reckner 2005). The search produced 260 relevant items. The vast majority of these referred to monuments having distinctly ethnic, religious, and military associations. Only 1 item in 260 had a labor history or class conflict dimension. This item described a series of attacks on a San Diego public park in the spring of 2003. The vandals defaced a statue of Cesar Chavez and a mural honoring Mexican workers who died trying to immigrate to the United States. However, the text of the article focused on the anti-Mexican dimension of the crime rather than its labor/class dimensions; that is, it reflected a racial rather than class consciousness.

A search of national and regional newspapers produced similar results: heavy reporting of desecrations at churches, cemeteries, and war memorials. We found only one report of vandalism of a labor-related marker, again involving Cesar Chavez. The incident involved the defacement of a marker sign for the Cesar Chavez Memorial Highway in 1999 near Corpus Christi in southern Texas. Here, the writer made reference to Chavez's labor activism but nonetheless emphasized the growth of a "wider Hispanic civil rights movement" as Chavez's legacy. A local politician who picketed with Chavez in the early 1970s expressed his shock and anger at the crime by comparing the hatefulness of the Chavez vandalism to that of the desecration of a Jewish cemetery. Thus, the event's significance was also conceptualized in distinctly ethnic and racial, rather than working-class, terms.

Of course, none of this is entirely surprising. Because of the progressive and triumphal nature of official public history (chapter 2)—a public history aided by the dominant American ideology of classlessness and often abetted by civic authorities and philanthropic industrialists—we should expect working-class history to be a hidden and/or displaced element in media reporting of monument vandalism, in the educational system, and in popular discourse generally (Walker 2003). American history textbooks tend to underplay Ludlow if mentioning it at all. As noted in chapter 5, our on-site interviews with visitors to the Ludlow Massacre Memorial are striking evidence of the event's status as hidden history.

Organized labor has long been aware that its history is under constant threat of erasure. Official history can be an overwhelming physical presence through historic markers, museums, and public ceremonies. Within two years of the massacre, miners were expressing concern that Ludlow would disappear from public memory (Walker 2003). The construction of the monument in 1918 was a deliberate effort to ensure that this would not occur. Over the years, unions and working-class communities have invested a surprising amount of effort in memorials and monuments to commemorate significant labor events. Memory takes continuous work. A monument soon drifts into invisibility through habitual viewing. The annual ceremonies at Ludlow serve to keep the meaning of the monument alive and constitute a shout against the silence. The need for Ludlow to be remembered is still a powerful refrain. For example, a recent song about Ludlow, on a compact disc put out to benefit the striking steelworkers in Pueblo, was entitled "Don't You Ever Forget." A recent pamphlet written by a local citizen implores us to *Remember Ludlow!* (Sampson 1999).

Thus, Ludlow is always in danger of being written out of national history. The question now is what politically engaged archaeologists with interests in collective action can do to reclaim and expand the space for labor history in public memory. Many eloquent and sensible pleas for engaging the unhappy events of our past have been made by historians. New Western historian Patricia Limerick has been in the forefront of this cause, suggesting that the more we critically deconstruct and demythologize the American past, the more we honor it (Limerick 1998). Others suggest that blind allegiance to "Fourth of July historiography"—one that celebrates heroic events and suppresses horrific ones—is not befitting a genuine democracy (for example, Dower 1995). Archaeologists have recently picked up on this theme, suggesting that more inclusive and better interpretations of the past are possible if we turn our attention to neglected histories, such as that of labor (Shackel 2004).

In the first edition of his book *Shadowed Ground*—the most comprehensive analysis of labor memorials and their place in the American commemorative landscape—Foote (1997) suggested that even though the overwhelming majority of significant events in American labor history remain unrecalled in official memory and unmarked on the nation's landscape, there was cause for optimism. The great industrialists are dead, we have a better awareness of how economic development threatens historic resources, and a 1991 U.S. House of Representatives report conceded that "the history of work and working people . . . is not adequately represented or preserved" in the United States (cited in Foote 1997: 303). These trends probably have something to do with the positive public response to our archaeological work since the Colorado Coalfield War Archaeological Project was initiated in 1997—coincidentally, the same year that Foote's book was published. The Colorado Historical Society has been very generous in its support of our project for a variety of reasons that likely include Ludlow's sensitivity to the immigrant story in the American West, especially as it concerns industrialization—a phenomenon that, as noted, still takes a backseat to homesteading and ranching in the area's official commemorative landscape.

These positive trends now show signs of reversing, however. In the second edition of his book, Foote (2003: 350) admits that since 1997, "efforts to expand the pantheon of labor leaders and the hall of honor of labor sites have not gone far." Part of the reason may be the continuing lack of direct involvement by organized labor. Foote (1997: 304) notes that organized labor needs to be more heavily involved as an active agent if local, "homegrown" markers are to become national markers having protected status. The late 1990s promised new and exciting activity on this front as labor and American universities began to entertain prospects for a reinvigorated relationship (Tomasky 1997; McGuire and Walker 1999). But since the national election of 2000, American labor has had to face other battles for survival. Moreover, long-standing competition between unions for members within the same industry has never been conducive to building the kind of unity that is required to create a national narrative around labor's history.

Another complicating factor at present is the resurgence of old-time triumphalism after September 11, 2001, and a renewed championing of national consensus history. The intellectual heirs of Lynne Cheney and William Bennett—aggressive opponents of pluralism and inclusiveness in public history during their successive tenures as chairs of the National Endowment for the Humanities between 1981 and 1993—are on the prowl (see also Shackel 2004). This time they are aided by a new conservative student activism on campus that is vigorously challenging what is portrayed as a dangerous liberal bias among university humanities faculty (Hebel 2004; Saitta 2006). The latter threatens to chill the climate for politically engaged teaching about American history and impede efforts to build a stronger relationship between the academy and organized labor. And although the Colorado Endowment for the Humanities remains supportive of projects in subaltern history, future teacher institutes are on hold while programs with greater purchase on the triumphal history of the American West—around the explorers John Wesley Powell and Lewis and Clark, for example—continue to run.

Coalfield Archaeology in the Service of Collective Action

So what is to be done in southeastern Colorado and other places where labor's often-bloody history is backgrounded or ignored? Professional historians and archaeologists converge in recommending national historic landmark (NHL) status for labor history sites (Green 2004; Shackel 2004). Such an effort is currently under way with respect to Ludlow (Green 2004), an effort in which we are participating. Attaining such status is easier said than done, especially at a time when, in keeping with the new triumphalism, NHL status is being rescinded for sites that potentially embarrass the reigning administration in Washington (Shackel 2004). Other issues surround who will control the interpretive message at NHL-designated sites. Minimally, we need to better tap into the "strong publics" (Fraser 1990; see also Green 2004) who closely identify with the events commemorated at historical sites and "have something to tell the rest of us about grief and loss, and the duty to remember" (Green 2004: 15).

A potential rub is that these strong publics often invoke vernacular histories of the past (Bodnar 1992). As noted in chapter 2, vernacular histories are local rather than national in orientation. They derive from the firsthand, everyday experience of people who were directly involved with history's events. Vernacular histories usefully challenge and even threaten the sacred and timeless nature of official history. But vernacular histories can be just as selective and exaggerated as official history in what gets remembered, and how.

Vernacular histories in southern Colorado—many proffered by members of the descendant community of coal miners—emphasize the militia's role in starting the shooting on April 20. They implicate the militia in many more atrocities against colonists on the day of the massacre and count many more casualties in the conflict.

Many vernacular accounts, for example, maintain that the Colorado militia used explosive bullets in their assault on the tent colony. The evidence from our excavations shows that this was not the case. The militia used standard military-issue steel-jacketed ball ammunition, examples of which were recovered from the site. We were also told by several local citizens that the number of Ludlow colonists killed in the massacre had been far higher—in the hundreds—and that the militia had dug a large pit in the middle of the camp and buried the bodies there. Our geophysical investigations and test excavations revealed no evidence for such a mass grave. When we heard such stories, we would explain why we thought that they were not true. How many minds we changed is not clear, but our explanations were always respectfully heard.

A safeguard against the potential excesses and polarizing effects of official and vernacular history is what we have termed critical history. Critical history understands that facts are selectively filtered and interpreted in keeping with theoretical preconceptions and existing social realities. With their unique database and hard-earned epistemological self-consciousness, archaeologists are well positioned to produce and disseminate critical history. In our public lectures about the coalfield war, we develop such a critical history while remaining sensitive to the fact that there is not just one alternative to official history, but many. We involve the purveyors of both official and vernacular histories in our summer teacher institutes, and we incorporate aspects of these accounts into tours and exhibits. In these contexts, we seek to build better history by comparing, contrasting, and exploring synergies between official, vernacular, and critical accounts. We do so in ways that are informed by archaeological data and faithful to the pragmatic weaving and hermeneutic fitting metaphors of Rorty and Hodder (described in chapters 2 and 3 of this book). This is much the better for building and mobilizing even stronger publics in the cause of less-selective and more-democratic national remembrance and for raising archaeology's stock as a socially relevant discipline.

The project is also contributing in more tangible, publicly visible ways to education, commemoration, and community building in the Colorado coal fields. Mindful of the silencing of labor history sites on the American commemorative landscape and directly confronted with minimalist public interpretation at Ludlow itself, one of our first achievements was to install a three-sided interpretive kiosk at the site that described the history, archaeology, and

Figure 7.5. Interpretive trail panels. Photograph by author.

legacy of the events that transpired there (Manajek 1999). The UMWA Local Women's Auxiliary had heavy input into kiosk design and urged a stronger connection between the Ludlow Massacre and contemporary labor struggles in the area. In so doing, they ensured that Ludlow was not consigned to a dead past, something that archaeological research at the site might suggest (Walker 2003: 75). We followed this up with a smaller historical marker for the Berwind coal camp modeled on the Corazon de Trinidad ("Heart of Trinidad") markers that celebrate Santa Fe Trail history in downtown Trinidad. The Berwind marker emphasizes the role played by Colorado's immigrants in the making of the industrial West. In June 2006, we installed an interpretive trail at the Ludlow memorial site, a full twelve panels that set forth a time line of the history, update the story told by archaeology, and locate the Ludlow drama in a wider landscape (figure 7.5). These interpretive materials do good work in offering counterclassic narratives to balance the triumphal, mythic narratives that have long informed western public history.

Figure 7.6. Restored
Ludlow monument,
2005. Photograph by
author.

Thus, the Colorado Coalfield War Archaeological Project has come a long
way since encountering that initial unnerving mix of descendant community
suspicion, bewilderment, and mild antagonism (chapter 2; Walker 2003).
Engagement and dialogue with this community has produced many uplift-
ing moments. In an article for *Archaeology* magazine—the discipline's main
pipeline to the middle class—Randy McGuire writes movingly of how striking Pueblo steelworkers, after a public lecture about archaeology at Ludlow,
insisted over his objections that we accept small but likely very precious donations of money to support the excavations (McGuire 2004). Indeed, the steelworkers were adamant that their money go to archaeological research rather
than to strike relief. On the occasion of the restored Ludlow monument's re-
dedication in 2005 (figure 7.6), union leaders announced that, as a result of
our efforts to publicize the story of Ludlow, we were now seen as "brothers and
sisters" in the struggle for workplace justice (Butero 2005).

Contact with the archaeology itself has produced other sorts of emotions and epiphanies. Upon viewing excavated artifacts, Yolanda Romero, president of the UMWA Local 9856 Women's Auxiliary commented, "Until now, we've only known what we've seen in photographs. But to see a real thing, an item that a person actually handled, really brings those people and that time to life . . . workers today are still fighting for some of the same protections the Ludlow miners wanted. People should know how far we've come and how far we still have to go" (*UMWJ* 1999: 13).

Such reactions to the work are professionally and personally fulfilling and suggest that we are having some success in building a distinctive emancipatory archaeology. They are all the more gratifying since the archaeological research that produced them did not require compromising explanatory goals or breaking faith with any of the epistemological or ethical principles that inform good scientific practice (see also Hall and Silliman 2006b). No doubt many other stories by project participants and community members could be told. My exposure to the artifacts excavated in the Italian family's tent at Locus 1 sensitized me to my own Italian ancestry and awakened a dormant ethnic pride (Saitta 2003). And as a relatively new father, I was deeply moved by the juxtaposition of baby spoons, diaper pins, and steel-jacketed militia bullets in the tent cellar at Feature 73, which brought home the sacrifices of the Ludlow strikers' families in a particularly poignant way.

Summary

The Colorado Coalfield War Archaeological Project is one that working people can relate to both intellectually and emotionally. It is one of the few archaeological projects in the United States that has spoken to the struggles of working-class people, past and present. The research questions and reporting style resonate with working-class sensibilities. Through public interpretation, site commemoration, and other outreach work, we have engaged an audience that has never heard of the Ludlow Massacre and also missed (or misunderstood) the history of U.S. labor conflict and its powerful legacy. In so doing, our work has shown how archaeology can contribute to a better understanding of the American experience: the historical origins of contemporary workplace rights, the tactics and strategies employed by capital and labor to negotiate their uneasy and at times explosive relationship, and the ability of ethnically diverse immigrant groups to come together for a great common cause. It also shows how and why the promise of an America premised on equality of opportunity and class mobility for all remains, for a significant number of our citizens, unfulfilled.

Whether this wider audience will be convinced of Ludlow's significance in the human struggle for workplace freedom and dignity remains to be seen (see Wood 2002b and Matthews 2005 for critiques of the Ludlow project's strategies of student and citizen engagement; also Nassaney 2004 for another example of how archaeology can serve the community through service-learning initiatives). For the moment, we content ourselves with the knowledge that we are politically engaged—that we are "in the game," to quote Hall (2004)—and the belief that our activities are cultivating some new audiences for archaeological work while simultaneously justifying archaeology's existence as an enterprise that serves the wider public good.

8

Critical Archaeology, Collective Action, and Disciplinary Futures

The studies of collective action described in this book are producing new knowledge about human agency in the past, while simultaneously engaging with various forms of collective action in the present. They help extend a tradition of thought that considers archaeological knowledge against a backdrop of contemporary processes and problems (for example, contributors to Buchli and Lucas 2001). In short, they have both explanatory and emancipatory power. In this conclusion I summarize why the archaeologies of collective action matter and where they might go from here.

Archaeologies of collective action matter, first and foremost, because they balance our view of the past. They foreground the contributions that various historically marginalized groups have made to the American experience. In so doing, they expand the cast of characters involved in the making of America. This contributes to better—more complete, more accurate, more democratic, even more humane—histories. This is so much the better for a discipline whose history and widely perceived status as a middle-class, leisure-time activity continually threatens it with irrelevance. As argued in chapter 2, the key to building these better histories is breaking with, or minimally putting a more pragmatic spin on, the realist epistemologies that currently unite practitioners across archaeology's theoretical spectrum. That is, we need to be as sensitive to how our practice articulates with ways of living as we are to how it advances ways of knowing. And this means measuring disciplinary progress less in terms of the accumulation of descriptive and explanatory knowledge (Hill 1991) and more in terms of our ability to respond to the needs of ever more inclusive groups of people (Rorty 1994: 81).

From a more critical, activist standpoint, archaeologies of collective action matter because they throw the inequalities of past and present into higher relief. In all cases, they destabilize and challenge claims that the social inequalities that divide us are rooted in ineluctable biologies or inevitable histories. The studies summarized here show the contingent quality of human histories and lifeworlds and, by extension, their changeability. As noted previously, contingency is an invitation and license to participate in history. Identifying the strategies of domination, resistance, and alliance building employed by differentially empowered agents and groups in the past allows us to evaluate their relative success and possible relevance to "insurgent oppositional movements" (Harvey 2000: 245) today.

Archaeological research in the southern Colorado coalfield has done less to provide specific guidance for such movements than underscore the challenge facing them. As with many other labor actions, the Ludlow strike was derailed by labor's inability to connect particular local struggles—what Williams (1989) calls "militant particularisms"—to a general struggle, that is, to link labor action at a variety of places in a way that leads to better resource control over larger spatial arenas. The lesson for organized labor is one that perhaps still needs to be learned, given the historical fractures experienced by the movement in 2005 (Greenhouse 2005). Namely, such solidarity can be achieved only by better negotiating between different place-specific demands, concerns, and aspirations, and in ways that can withstand both the strain produced by internal competing visions and the corruptions brought by more powerful outside interests.

Having explored how collective action works with respect to race, gender, and class in past historical contexts, where might a critical archaeology push the study of collective action in the future? What comes next (Matthews, Leone, and Jordan 2002: 132)? Of course, there are as many visions for archaeology's future as there are practitioners of the craft. Given the documented effectivity and complex interpenetrability of race, gender, ethnicity, sexuality, and other identities in social life, good arguments can be made for any one of them as a useful entry point for critical social analysis. But also given what some see as the strategic limitations of identity politics as usual for creating change (Brubaker and Cooper 2000; McGuire and Wurst 2003), it seems useful to have a more serious discussion about the relative tactical merits of particular entry points vis-à-vis the societal challenges of the present.

Here, I do nothing more than make a plea for greater attention to class. Class is very much at issue in contemporary America, not just in the mining industry but in a number of industries. Even today's mainstream press is pointing out that class divisions in America are as deep, and the opportunities for social mobility as limited, as ever (Scott and Leonhardt 2005). Thus, class poses real existential problems for Americans. As a subject for scholarly analysis, class is still avoided, obscured, or ignored, as much in anthropology and archaeology as in any other discipline (Knapp 1996; Duke and Saitta 1998; Ortner 1998; Wurst and Fitts 1999; Durrenberger 2001; Wurst 2006). Recall that only very recently has capitalism emerged as an explicit object of study in historical archaeology. The argument here is that we are already used to think-ing about ourselves in nonclass—race, sex, gender, and ethnic group—terms. What might happen if we begin thinking about our social lives in explicitly class terms, that is, if we map our class positions in life by using the production and distribution of human social labor as the touchstone for analysis, instead of the usual touchstones of wealth, status, property, or authority? What kinds of fruitful collaborations and alliances might then take shape across gender, race, ethnicity, sexuality, and the other identities that divide us? This call is not to implicate class as the most important structuring principle of human life in any sort of ontological or causal sense. It is merely to consider the possible tactical advantages of focusing on class as a way to advance progressive social change.

This class-theoretical approach to identity politics gains as a compelling and potentially unifying strategy if we accept that the study of class—again, understood as a relational phenomenon structured around how social labor is produced and distributed in society—is not limited to the modern world. Elsewhere I have advocated the importance of class as an intellectual tool for cross-cultural and transhistorical analysis and comparison (Saitta 2005). A long-standing tendency within anthropology and archaeology to insist on a distinction between class and nonclass societies (for example, Spriggs 1984) unnecessarily hamstrings explanatory theory and, I would argue, agendas for emancipatory change. Class as understood here allows us to consider the com-mon existential problems that tie working people in all societies and historical epochs together and the variety of ways that they coped with these problems. The vision is for a *comparative* archaeology that highlights the differences between ancient and modern lifeways and "thoughtworlds" as concerns the social organization of production (see also Orser 2001). Minimally, such an archaeology could contrast the drudgery, monotony, isolation, anxiety, and alienation of much industrial capitalist production with the arguably richer forms of economic and cultural life that existed before alarm clocks and gen-teel consumer culture. Part of this project would require—following the lead of Lukacs (1971; see also Leone 1995)—using archaeology to show how groups who have learned (via the usual identity politics) to see themselves as different in a variety of nonclass ways share some common class experiences (see also Harvey 2000).

Whatever identity axis is determined to be strategically useful, the other tactical challenge is to more broadly disseminate, in the public arena, the dis-tinctive archaeological knowledge that we take to have emancipatory import. As noted in chapter 7, post-9/11 resurgence of progressivist and triumpha-list thought about American history—transparently offered by our leaders as an antidote to criticisms of American exceptionalism and even as a sinister warning to the critics themselves—threaten to swamp recent democratizing trends in public history, archaeology, and memory. Emancipatory archaeologies must do a couple of things to counter these reactionary trends. One is to better engage with alternative archaeologies, including those "fringe," "cult," or "pseudo" archaeologies that archaeologists tend to dismiss out of hand (Holtorf 2005). While "policing prehistory" for fact abuse by extraterrestrial diffusionists and goddess worshipers has its place (see Brumfiel 2003 on archaeologists as "chronocops"), crusades and jihads against the archaeological "other" can hurt more than help. In a consideration of the epistemological and social statuses of mainstream and fringe archaeologies, Holtorf (2005: 548) offers some food for thought: the "significance of archaeology may lie less in any specific insight gained about the past than in the process of engaging with the material remains of the past." Holtorf's plea, like Rorty's, is for "critical understanding and dialogue" (Holtorf 2005: 550) rather than for patronizing or dismissive polemics. In other words, the call is for a conversation that weaves and reweaves ideas in ways that "enlarge the scope of us" (Rorty 1991: 38) without succumbing to Latour's "frantic disorderly mob" (Latour 1999: 22; for an alternative view, see Fagan and Feder 2006).

The other part of the outreach challenge is to experiment with alternative modes of communication and representation if we are to achieve the kind of unforced agreement (Rorty 1989) among relevant constituencies that is a prerequisite for effective collective action. As Harvey (2000) notes, such translations of knowledge and political aspirations between people are crucial for the success of any insurgent oppositional movement. Wilkie (2005) notes that historical archaeology has been on the leading edge of knowledge translation in the field, with its pioneering exploration of more self-reflexive narrative and multivocal modes of exposition (for example, Praetzellis and Praetzellis 2001; contributors to Joyce 2002). If we want to change the middle-class character of the discipline and create more potent communities for change—new fields of social action—we need better ways to integrate academic and nonacademic audiences and sensibilities. Wilkie (2005) also contextualizes this virtue of historical archaeology in a narrower call for more and better communication between professional historical and prehistoric archaeologists. For a variety of reasons, each of the two camps tends to stick to its own turf, rarely entering into fruitful debate. But the two must converse, especially if the cause of the comparative, class-theoretical archaeology called for here and implicated as a need by others is to be advanced. Wilkie's takeaway message, as well as Paynter's (2000b), is a good one: *all* archaeology is historical archaeology.

The combined message of processual and postprocessual, prehistoric and historic archaeology—one substantiated by lots of empirical work—is that societies live far from a static equilibrium. They are always balanced on an edge, requiring constant inputs of energy, meaning, and material culture to stay together. Archaeology, because of its particular middle-class position and roughly corresponding intellectual agenda, is a disciplinary practice that is also always poised on a brink—that of irrelevancy. As emphasized throughout this book, the battle today is first and foremost for the hearts and minds of citizens having pressing existential concerns and relatively short memories. A better understanding of collective action in history—one focused on meaningful differences, deepened and enriched by archaeological knowledge, and better translated as a piece of public memory—promises interventions that can benefit society and help perpetuate our craft as a distinctive contributor to public discourse and debate.

References

Abrams, James. 1994. Lost Frames of Reference: Sightings of History and Memory in Pennsylvania's Documentary Landscape. In *Conserving Culture: A New Discourse on Heritage,* ed. M. Hufford, 24–38. Urbana: University of Illinois Press.

Adams, Graham. 1966. *The Age of Industrial Violence, 1910–1915: The Activities and Findings of the U.S. Commission on Industrial Relations.* New York: Columbia University Press.

Albright, J. 1975. The Governor, the Secretary of War, and the Colorado Coal Strike. Manuscript on file at the Colorado Historical Society, Denver.

Anyon, Roger, T. J. Ferguson, Loretta Jackson, Lillie Lane, and Philip Vicenti. 1997. Native American Oral Tradition and Archaeology: Issues of Structure, Relevance, and Respect. In *Native Americans and Archaeologists,* ed. N. Swidler, K. Dongoske, R. Anyon, and A. Downer, 77–87. Walnut Creek, Calif.: AltaMira Press.

Appleby, Joyce, Lynn Hunt, and Margaret Jacob. 1994. *Telling the Truth about History.* New York: W. W. Norton.

Barrett, John. 2001. Agency, the Duality of Structure, and the Problem of the Archaeological Record. In *Archaeological Theory Today,* ed. I. Hodder, 141–64. Cambridge, U.K.: Polity Press.

Beaudry, Mary, Lauren Cook, and Stephen Mrozowski. 1991. Artifacts and Active Voices: Material Culture as Social Discourse. In *The Archaeology of Inequality,* ed. R. McGuire and R. Paynter, 150–91. Oxford, U.K.: Basil Blackwell.

Beaudry, Mary, and Stephen Mrozowski. 2001. Cultural Space and Worker Identity in the Company City: Nineteenth Century Lowell, Massachusetts. In *The Archaeology of Urban Landscapes: Explorations in Slumland,* ed. A. Mayne and T. Murray, 118–31. Cambridge: Cambridge University Press.

Bee, Tanja. 1997. Coal Miner's Memorial: Five Year Effort Culminates in Dedication of Memorial in Honor of Area's Miners. *Trinidad Chronicle-News,* August 4.

Beik, Mildred. 1999. Commemoration and Contestation: Remembering the Unsung Miners of Windber, Pennsylvania. Paper presented at the North American Labor History Conference, Detroit, Michigan.

Bernstein, Richard. 1988. *The New Constellation.* Cambridge, Mass.: MIT Press.

Beshoar, Barron. 1942. *Out of the Depths.* Denver: Colorado Historical Commission and Denver Trades and Labor Assembly.

Binford, Lewis R. 1962. Archaeology as Anthropology. *American Antiquity* 28: 217–25.

———. 1982a. Meaning, Inference, and the Material Record. In *Ranking, Resource, and Exchange,* ed. C. Renfrew and S. Shennan, 160–63. Cambridge: Cambridge University Press.

———. 1982b. Objectivity-Explanation-Archaeology, 1981. In *Theory and Explanation in Archaeology,* ed. C. Renfrew, M. Rowlands, and B. Segraves, 125–38. New York: Academic Press.

———. 1987. Researching Ambiguity: Frames of Reference and Site Structure. In *Method and Theory for Activity Area Research,* ed. S. Kent, 449–512. New York: Columbia University Press.

Bodnar, John. 1992 *Remaking America: Public Memory, Commemoration, and Patriotism in the Twentieth Century.* Princeton, N.J.: Princeton University Press.

Bourdieu, Pierre. 1977. *Outline of a Theory of Practice.* Cambridge: Cambridge University Press.

Brant, John. 1996. Unemployment: The Theme Park. *New York Times Magazine,* January 28, 46–47.

Braun, David. 1991. Are There Cross-Cultural Regularities in Tribal Social Practices? In *Between Bands and States,* ed. S. Gregg, 423–44. Carbondale, Ill.: Center for Archaeological Investigations.

Braverman, Harry. 1974. *Labor and Monopoly Capital.* New York: Monthly Review Press.

Brooke, James. 1998. West Celebrates Mining's Past, But Not Its Future. *New York Times,* October 4.

Brubaker, Rogers, and Frederick Cooper. 2000. Beyond "Identity." *Theory and Society* 29: 1–47.

Brumfiel, Elizabeth. 1992. Distinguished Lecture in Archaeology: Breaking and Entering the Ecosystem—Gender, Class, and Faction Steal the Show. *American Anthropologist* 94: 551–67.

———. 2003. It's a Material World: History, Artifacts, and Anthropology. *Annual Review of Anthropology* 32: 205–23.

Buchli, Victor. 2004. Material Cultures: Current Problems. In *A Companion to Social Archaeology,* ed. L. Meskell and R. Preucel, 179–94. Oxford, U.K.: Blackwell Publishing.

Buchli, Victor, and Gavin Lucas, eds. 2001. *Archaeologies of the Contemporary Past.* London: Routledge.

Butero, Bob. 2005. Remarks at the Ludlow Memorial Service, Ludlow, Colorado, June 5.

Caputo, Silvio. 1984. *The Death of Spring.* Port Washington, N.Y.: Ashley Books.

Carson, Rachel. 1962. *Silent Spring.* Boston: Houghton Mifflin.

Clark, Geoffrey. 1998. NAGPRA, the Conflict between Science and Religion, and the Political Consequences. *Society for American Archaeology Bulletin* 16(5): 22.

Clyne, Rick. 1999. *Coal People: Life in Southern Colorado's Company Towns, 1890–1930.* Denver: Colorado Historical Society.

Colorado Special Board of Officers. 1915. *Ludlow: Being the Report of the Special Board of Officers Appointed by the Governor of Colorado to Investigate and Determine the Facts with Reference to the Armed Conflict between the Colorado National Guard and Certain Persons Engaged in the Coal-mining Strike at Ludlow, Colorado, April 20, 1914.* Denver.

Conkey, Margaret. 1989. The Place of Material Culture Studies in Contemporary Anthropology. In *Perspectives on Anthropological Collections from the American Southwest*, ed. A. Hedlund, 13–30. Tempe: Arizona State University.

Cowgill, George. 1975. On the Causes and Consequences of Ancient and Modern Population Changes. *American Anthropologist* 77: 505–25.

Crawford, Margaret. 1995. *Building the Workingman's Paradise: The Design of American Company Towns*. London: Verso.

Cronon, William, George Miles, and Jay Gitlin. 1992. Becoming West: Toward a New Meaning for Western History. In *Under an Open Sky: Rethinking America's Western Past*, ed. W. Cronon, G. Miles, and J. Gitlin, 3–27. New York: W. W. Norton.

Curtin, D. J. 1991. Structuring History: Perceptions of American Cowboy Culture. Master's thesis, Binghamton University, Binghamton, N.Y.

Deetz, James. 1993. *Flowerdew Hundred: The Archaeology of a Virginia Plantation, 1619–1864*. Charlottesville: University of Virginia Press.

Delarbre, Raul. 2003. Ludlow, 1914. *La Cronica de Hoy*. June 30.

Delle, James, Stephen Mrozowski, and Robert Paynter. 2000a. Introduction. In *Lines That Divide: Historical Archaeologies of Race, Class, and Gender*, xi–xxxi. Knoxville: University of Tennessee Press.

———, eds. 2000b. *Lines That Divide: Historical Archaeologies of Race, Class, and Gender*. Knoxville: University of Tennessee Press.

Deutsch, Claudia. 2006. Company Owner Says Cost Cutting Didn't Lead to Mine Explosion. *New York Times*, January 5.

Deutsch, Sarah. 1986. *No Separate Refuge: Culture, Class, and Gender on an Anglo-Hispanic Frontier in the American Southwest, 1880–1940*. New York: Oxford University Press.

Dewey, John. 1917. The Need for a Recovery of Philosophy. In *Pragmatism: A Reader*, ed. L. Menand, 219–32. New York: Vintage Books.

Dobres, Marcia-Ann. 2000. *Technology and Social Agency*. Oxford, U.K.: Blackwell Publishers.

Dobres, Marcia-Ann, and John Robb, eds. 2000. *Agency in Archaeology*. London: Routledge.

———. 2005. "Doing" Agency: Introductory Remarks on Methodology. *Journal of Archaeological Method and Theory* 12: 159–66.

Donachy, Patrick. 1989. *A Rendezvous with Shame*. Trinidad, Colo.: Inkwell.

Dornan, Jennifer. 2002. Agency and Archaeology: Past, Present, and Future Directions. *Journal of Archaeological Method and Theory* 9: 303–29.

Dower, J. 1995. How a Genuine Democracy Should Celebrate Its Past. *Chronicle of Higher Education*, June 16.

Duke, Philip, ed. 1999. *Affiliation Conference on Ancestral Peoples of the Four Corners Region, Papers and Transcripts*, vols. 1–3. Durango, Colo.: Fort Lewis College and National Park Service.

Duke, Philip, and Dean J. Saitta. 1998. An Emancipatory Archaeology for the Working Class. *Assemblage* 4. http://www.shef.ac.uk/~assem/44duk_sai.html.

Dunnell, Robert. 1989. Aspects of the Application of Evolutionary Theory in Archaeology. In *Archaeological Thought in America,* ed. C. C. Lamberg-Karlovsky, 35–49. Cambridge: Cambridge University Press.

Durrenberger, Paul. 2001. On Class. *Anthropology Newsletter,* September.

Eagleton, Terry. 1996. *The Illusion of Postmodernism.* Oxford, U.K.: Blackwell.

Echo-Hawk, Roger. 2000. Ancient History in the New World: Integrating Oral Traditions and the Archaeological Record in Deep Time. *American Antiquity* 65: 267–90.

Ehrlich, Paul. 1968. *The Population Bomb.* New York: Ballantine Books.

Ember, Carol, and Melvin Ember. 1992. Resource Unpredictability, Mistrust, and War. *Journal of Conflict Resolution* 36: 242–62.

Fabian, Johannes. 1994. Ethnographic Objectivity Revisited: From Rigor to Vigor. In *Rethinking Objectivity,* ed. A. Megill, 81–108. Durham, N.C.: Duke University Press.

Fagan, Garret G., and Kenneth L. Feder. 2006. Crusading Against Straw Men: An Alternative View of Alternative Archaeologies: Response to Holtorf (2005). *World Archaeology* 38: 718–29.

Ferguson, Leland. 1991. Struggling with Pots in South Carolina. In *The Archaeology of Inequality,* ed. R. Paynter and R. McGuire, 28–39. London: Blackwell.

———. 1992. *Uncommon Ground: Archaeology and Early African America.* Washington, D.C.: Smithsonian Institution Press.

———. 1999. "The Cross Is a Magic Sign": Marks on Eighteenth-Century Bowls from South Carolina. In *"I Too Am America": Archaeological Studies of African-American Life,* ed. T. Singleton, 116–31, Charlottesville: University Press of Virginia.

Fetty, C. R., III. 2001. Don't You Ever Forget. In *Strike Force, Knights of the Union.* Pueblo, Colo.: Canis Minor Records.

Firestone, David. 2001. 4 Dead and 9 Missing in a Pair of Alabama Mine Blasts. *New York Times,* September 25.

Fitts, Robert K. 2002. Becoming American: The Archaeology of an Italian Immigrant. *Historical Archaeology* 36 (2): 1–17.

Foner, Philip. 1980. *History of the Labor Movement in the United States,* vol. 5, *The AFL in the Progressive Era, 1910–1915.* New York: International Publishers.

Foote, Kenneth. 1997. *Shadowed Ground: America's Landscapes of Violence and Tragedy.* 1st ed. Austin: University of Texas Press.

———. 2003. *Shadowed Ground: America's Landscapes of Violence and Tragedy.* 2nd ed. Austin: University of Texas Press.

Ford, Richard. 1973. Archaeology Serving Humanity. In *Research and Theory in Current Archaeology,* ed. C. Redman, 83–93. New York: Wiley.

Foucault, Michel. 1979. *Discipline and Punish.* New York: Vintage Books.

———. 1980. *Power and Knowledge.* New York: Pantheon.

Fraser, Nancy. 1990. Rethinking the Public Sphere: A Contribution to the Critique of Actually Existing Democracy. *Social Text* 25/26: 56–80.

Funari, Pedro, Martin Hall, and Sian Jones, eds. 1999. *Historical Archaeology: Back from the Edge.* London: Routledge.

Gathercole, Peter, and David Lowenthal, eds. 1990. *The Politics of the Past.* London: Unwin Hyman.

Geertz, Clifford. 1973. *The Interpretation of Cultures.* New York: Basic Books.

———. 1983. *Local Knowledge: Further Essays in Interpretive Anthropology.* New York: Basic Books.

Gell, Alfred. 1998. *Art and Agency: An Anthropological Theory.* Oxford, U.K.: Clarendon Press.

Gero, Joan, and Margaret Conkey, eds. 1991. *Engendering Archaeology.* Oxford, U.K.: Basil Blackwell.

Gero, Joan, David Lacy, and Michael Blakey, eds. 1983. *The Socio-politics of Archaeology.* University of Massachusetts Anthropological Research Report Series 23. Amherst.

Giddens, Anthony. 1979. *Central Problems in Social Theory.* London: Macmillan.

———. 1984. *The Constitution of Society: Outline of a Theory of Structuration.* Cambridge, U.K.: Polity Press.

Gitelman, Howard. 1988. *Legacy of the Ludlow Massacre: A Chapter in American Industrial Relations.* Philadelphia: University of Pennsylvania Press.

Gosden, Chris. 2001. Postcolonial Archaeology: Issues of Culture, Identity, and Knowledge. In *Archaeological Theory Today,* ed. I. Hodder, 241–61. Cambridge, U.K.: Polity Press.

———. 2004. The Past and Foreign Countries: Colonial and Post-colonial Archaeology and Anthropology. In *A Companion to Social Archaeology,* ed. L. Meskell and R. Preucel, 161–78. Oxford, U.K.: Blackwell Publishing.

Gray, Amie. 2005. *Contested Ideals: Cultural Citizenship at the Ludlow Tent Colony.* Master's thesis, Department of Anthropology, University of Denver.

Green, Arlee. 1995. Labor Landmarks: Past and Present. *Labor's Heritage* 6: 26–53.

Green, James. 2004. Crime against Memory at Ludlow. *Labor: Studies in Working Class History of the Americas* 1: 9–16.

Greenhouse, Steven. 2005. Labor Debates the Future of a Fractured Movement. *New York Times,* July 27.

Gutman, Herbert. 1977. *Work, Culture, and Society.* New York: Vintage Books.

Habermas, Jurgen. 1971. *Knowledge and Human Interests.* London: Heinemann.

Hall, Martin. 2004. Keynote Address. Contemporary and Historical Archaeology Theory Conference, Leicester, England.

Hall, Martin, and Stephen W. Silliman, eds. 2006a. *Historical Archaeology.* Oxford, U.K.: Blackwell Publishing.

———. 2006b. Introduction: Archaeology of the Modern World. In *Historical Archaeology,* ed. M. Hall and S. Silliman, 1–19. Oxford, U.K.: Blackwell Publishing.

Hallam, Elizabeth, and Jenny Hockey. 2001. *Death, Memory, and Material Culture.* Oxford, U.K.: Berg.

Hardesty, Donald. 1998. Power and the Industrial Mining Community in the American West. In *Social Approaches to an Industrial Past,* ed. A. B. Knapp, V. Pigott, and E. Herbert, 81–96. London: Routledge.

Harvey, David. 1973. *Social Justice and the City.* London: Arnold.

———. 2000. *Spaces of Hope.* Berkeley: University of California Press.

Hebel, Sara. 2004. Patrolling Professors' Politics. *Chronicle of Higher Education,* February 13.

Hegmon, Michelle. 2003. Setting Theoretical Egos Aside: Issues and Theory in North American Archaeology. *American Antiquity* 68: 213–43.

Heidegger, Martin. 1927. *Being and Time.* San Francisco: Harper.

Hill, James, ed. 1977. *The Explanation of Prehistoric Change.* Santa Fe, N. Mex.: School of American Research.

———. 1991. Archaeology and the Accumulation of Knowledge. In *Processual and Postprocessual Archaeologies: Multiple Ways of Knowing the Past,* ed. R. Preucel, 42–53. Carbondale, Ill.: Center for Archaeological Investigations.

Hodder, Ian. 1982a. Theoretical Archaeology: A Reactionary View. In *Symbolic and Structural Archaeology,* ed. I. Hodder, 1–16. Cambridge: Cambridge University Press.

———. 1982b. *Symbolic and Structural Archaeology.* Cambridge: Cambridge University Press.

———. 1982c. *Symbols in Action.* Cambridge: Cambridge University Press.

———. 1991a. *Reading the Past.* Cambridge: Cambridge University Press.

———. 1991b. The Decoration of Containers: An Ethnographic and Historical Study. In *Ceramic Ethnoarchaeology,* ed. W. Longacre, 71–94. Tucson: University of Arizona Press.

———. 1991c. Interpretive Archaeology and Its Role. *American Antiquity* 56: 7–18.

———. 1999. *The Archaeological Process.* Oxford, U.K.: Blackwell.

———. 2001a. Introduction: A Review of Contemporary Theoretical Debates in Archaeology. In *Archaeological Theory Today,* ed. I. Hodder, 1–13. Cambridge, U.K.: Polity Press.

———, ed. 2001b. *Archaeological Theory Today.* Cambridge, U.K.: Polity Press.

———. 2004. The "Social" in Archaeological Theory: An Historical and Contemporary Perspective. In *A Companion to Social Archaeology,* ed. L. Meskell and R. Preucel, 23–42. Oxford, U.K.: Blackwell Publishing.

Hodder, Ian, and Scott Hutson. 2003. *Reading the Past.* 3rd ed. Cambridge: Cambridge University Press.

Holtorf, Cornelius. 2005. Beyond Crusades: How (Not) to Engage with Alternative Archaeologies. *World Archaeology* 37: 544–51.

Jacobson, Michael. 2002. Ideological Clash: A Study of Experience in the Colorado Coalfield War 1913–1914. Master's thesis, Department of Anthropology, Binghamton University, Binghamton, N.Y.

———. 2006. The Rise and Fall of Place: The Development of a Sense of Place and Community in Colorado's Southern Coalfields, 1890–1930. Doctoral dissertation, Department of Anthropology, Binghamton University, Binghamton, N.Y.

Jameson, Elizabeth. 1998. *All That Glitters: Class, Conflict, and Community in Cripple Creek.* Urbana: University of Illinois Press.

Jasper, Joanne. 1996. *Turn of the Century American Dinnerware: 1880s to 1920s.* Paducah, Ky.: Collector Books.

Johnson, Matthew. 1989. Conceptions of Agency in Archaeological Interpretation. *Journal of Anthropological Archaeology* 8: 189–211.

———. 1999. *Archaeological Theory: An Introduction.* Oxford, U.K.: Blackwell.

Joyce, Rosemary, ed. 2002. *The Languages of Archaeology.* Oxford, U.K.: Blackwell.

Karaim, Reed. 1997. Time Out of Mine: Airstreams, Aging Hippies, and UFOs Meet the Ghosts of Miners Past in a Well-Preserved Arizona Desert Town. *Preservation* (March/April): 83–86.

Kloppenberg, James. 1996. Pragmatism: An Old Name for Some New Ways of Thinking? *Journal of American History* 83: 100–138.

Knapp, Bernard. 1996. Archaeology without Gravity: Postmodernism and the Past. *Journal of Archaeological Method and Theory* 3: 127–58.

Kohl, Philip, and Clare Fawcett. 1995. *Nationalism, Politics, and the Practice of Archaeology.* Cambridge: Cambridge University Press.

Kosso, Peter. 1991. Method in Archaeology: Middle-Range Theory as Hermeneutics. *American Antiquity* 56: 621–27.

LaRoche, Cheryl, and Michael Blakey. 1997. Seizing Intellectual Power: The Dialogue at the New York African Burial Ground. *Historical Archaeology* 31: 84–106.

Latour, Bruno. 1999. *Pandora's Hope: Essays on the Reality of Science Studies.* Cambridge, Mass.: Harvard University Press.

Lekson, Stephen. 2002. War in the Southwest, War in the World. *American Antiquity* 67: 607–24.

Leone, Mark. 1984. Interpreting Ideology in Historical Archaeology: Using the Rules of Perspective in the William Paca Garden in Annapolis, Maryland. In *Ideology, Power, and Prehistory,* ed. D. Miller and C. Tilley, 25–35. Cambridge: Cambridge University Press.

———. 1986. Symbolic, Structural, and Critical Archaeology. In *American Archaeology Past and Future,* ed. D. Meltzer, D. Fowler, and J. Sabloff, 415–38. Washington, D.C.: Smithsonian Institution Press.

———. 1988. The Georgian Order as the Order of Merchant Capitalism in Annapolis, Maryland. In *The Recovery of Meaning: Historical Archaeology in the Eastern United States,* ed. M. Leone and P. Potter, 235–61. Washington, D.C.: Smithsonian Institution Press.

———. 1995. A Historical Archaeology of Capitalism. *American Anthropologist* 97: 251–68.

Leone, Mark, and Parker Potter Jr., eds. 1988. *The Recovery of Meaning: Historical Archaeology in the Eastern United States.* Washington, D.C.: Smithsonian Institution Press.

———, eds. 1999. *Historical Archaeologies of Capitalism.* New York: Plenum Press.

Leone, Mark, Parker Potter Jr., and Paul Shackel. 1987. Toward a Critical Archaeology. *Current Anthropology* 28: 283–302.

Leone, Mark, and Paul Shackel. 1987. Forks, Clocks and Power. In *Mirror and Metaphor,* ed. D. Ingersoll and G. Bronitsky, 45–61. Lapham, Md.: University Press of America.

Limerick, Patricia. 1987. *The Legacy of Conquest.* New York: Norton.

———. 1991. What On Earth Is the New Western History? In *Trails: Toward a New Western History,* ed. P. Limerick, C. Milner, and C. Rankin, 81–88. Lawrence: University Press of Kansas.

———. 1998. Hard Look at Heroes. *Denver Post,* p. G-01, June 7.

Little, Barbara. 1994. People with History: An Update on Historical Archaeology in the United States. *Journal of Archaeological Method and Theory* 1: 5–40.

———. 1997. Expressing Ideology without a Voice, or Obfuscation and the Enlightenment. *International Journal of Historical Archaeology* 1: 225–41.

Lomaomvaya, Micah, and T. J. Ferguson. 2003. Hisatqatsit Aw Maamatslalwa—Comprehending Our Past Lifeways: Thoughts about a Hopi Archaeology. In *Indigenous People and Archaeology*, ed. T. Peck, E. Siegfried, and G. Oetelaar, 43–51. Calgary: Archaeological Association of the University of Calgary.

Long, Priscilla. 1985. The Women of the Colorado Fuel and Iron Strike. In *Women, Work and Protest: A Century of U.S. Women's Labor History*, ed. R. Milkman, 62–85. London: Routledge and Kegan Paul.

———. 1989a. *Where the Sun Never Shines: A History of America's Bloody Coal Industry*. New York: Paragon House.

———. 1989b. The Voice of the Gun: Colorado's Great Coalfield War of 1913–1914. *Labor's Heritage* 1: 4–23.

Lowenthal, David. 1996. *Possessed by the Past: The Heritage Crusade and the Spoils of History*. New York: Free Press.

Ludlow Collective. 2001. Archaeology of the Colorado Coal Field War, 1913–1914. In *Archaeologies of the Contemporary Past*, ed. V. Buchli and G. Lucas, pp. 94–107. London: Routledge Press.

Lukacs, Georg. 1971. Reification and the Consciousness of the Proletariat. In *History and Class Consciousness*, trans. R. Livingstone, 83–222. Cambridge, Mass.: MIT Press.

Lynott, Mark, and Alison Wylie, eds. 2000. *Ethics in American Archaeology*. Washington, D.C.: Society for American Archaeology.

Manajek, Kim. 1999. Ludlow Massacre Interpretive Kiosk. Master's thesis, University of Denver, Denver, Colorado.

Margolis, Eric. 1985. Western Coal Mining as a Way of Life: An Oral History of the Colorado Coal Miners to 1914. *Journal of the West* 24 (3).

———. 2000. "Life Is Life": One Family's Struggle in the Southern Colorado Coalfields. *Colorado Heritage* (summer): 30–47.

———. n.d. Life Is Life: A Mining Family in the West. http://courses.ed.asu.edu/margolis/life/homepageexp.htm#_edn1.

Margolis, Eric, and Ronald L. MacMahan. 1975. Interview with Mike Livoda. November, Denver, Colorado. Audio tape 130-D. Transcript page 91. Transcripts and tapes filed at the Archives, University of Colorado Library, Boulder, Colorado.

Marquardt, William. 1992. Dialectical Archaeology. In *Archaeological Method and Theory*, vol. 4, ed. M. Schiffer, 101–40. Tucson: University of Arizona Press.

Marx, Karl. 1963. *The Eighteenth Brumaire of Louis Bonaparte*. New York: International Publishers.

Matthews, Christopher. 2005. Public Dialectics: Marxist Reflection in Archaeology. *Historical Archaeology* 39: 26–44.

Matthews, Christopher, Mark Leone, and Kurt Jordan. 2002. The Political Economy of Archaeological Cultures. *Journal of Social Archaeology* 2: 109–34.

McDavid, Carol. 1997. Descendants, Decisions, and Power: The Public Interpretation of the Archaeology of the Levi Jordan Plantation. *Historical Archaeology* 31: 114–31.

McGovern, George, and Leonard Guttridge. 1972. *The Great Coalfield War*. Boston: Houghton Mifflin.

McGuire, Randall. 2004. Colorado Coalfield Massacre. *Archaeology* 57 (6): 62–70.

McGuire, Randall, and R. Paynter, eds. 1991. *The Archaeology of Inequality*. London: Basil Blackwell.

McGuire, Randall, and Paul Reckner. 2002. The Unromantic West: Labor, Capital, and Struggle. *Historical Archaeology* 36: 44–58.

McGuire, Randall, and Mark Walker. 1999. Class Confrontations in Archaeology. *Historical Archaeology* 33: 159–83.

McGuire, Randall, and LouAnn Wurst. 2002. Struggling with the Past. *International Journal of Historical Archaeology* 6: 85–94.

Megill, Alan. 1994. Introduction: Four Senses of Objectivity. In *Rethinking Objectivity*, ed. A. Megill, 1–20. Durham, N.C.: Duke University Press.

Meltzer, David. 1981. Ideology and Material Culture. In *Modern Material Culture: The Archaeology of Us*, ed. M. Schiffer, 113–25. New York: Academic Press.

Menand, Louis. 1997. An Introduction to Pragmatism. In *Pragmatism*, ed. L. Menand, xi–xxxiv. New York: Vintage.

Meskell, Lynn, and Robert Preucel, eds. 2004a. *A Companion to Social Archaeology*. Oxford, U.K.: Blackwell Publishing.

———. 2004b. Knowledges. In *A Companion to Social Archaeology*, ed. L. Meskell and R. Preucel, 3–22. Oxford, U.K.: Blackwell Publishing.

———. 2004c. Politics. In *A Companion to Social Archaeology*, ed. L. Meskell and R. Preucel, 315–34. Oxford, U.K.: Blackwell Publishing.

———. 2004d. Identities. In *A Companion to Social Archaeology*, ed. L. Meskell and R. Preucel, 121–41. Oxford, U.K.: Blackwell Publishing.

Miller, Daniel, and Christopher Tilley, eds. 1984a. *Ideology, Power, and Prehistory*. Cambridge: Cambridge University Press.

———. 1984b. Ideology, Power, and Long-Term Social Change. In *Ideology, Power, and Prehistory*, ed. D. Miller and C. Tilley, 147–52. Cambridge: Cambridge University Press.

Miller, Daniel, Michael Rowlands, and Christopher Tilley. 1989. Introduction. In *Domination and Resistance*, ed. D. Miller, M. Rowlands, and C. Tilley, 1–26. London: Unwin Hyman.

Mondale, Clarence. 1994. Conserving a Problematic Past. In *Conserving Culture: A New Discourse on Heritage*, ed. M. Hufford, 15–23. Urbana: University of Illinois Press.

Moore, Summer. 2007. Working Parents and the Material Culture of Victorianism: Children's Toys at the Ludlow Tent Colony. In *The Archaeology of Class War*, edited by Randall McGuire and Karin Larkin. Boulder: University of Colorado Press.

Morgan, Lewis Henry. 1877. *Ancient Society*. New York: Labor Press.

Mrozowski, Stephen. 1991. Landscapes of Inequality. In *The Archaeology of Inequality*, ed. R. McGuire and R. Paynter, 79–101. Oxford, U.K.: Basil Blackwell.

Mullins, Paul. 1999a. *Race and Affluence: An Archaeology of African America and Consumer Culture*. New York: Plenum.

———. 1999b. "A Bold and Gorgeous Front": The Contradictions of African America and Consumer Culture. In *Historical Archaeologies of Capitalism*, ed. M. Leone and P. Potter, 169–93. New York: Plenum Press.

———. 2004. Ideology, Power, and Capitalism: The Historical Archaeology of Consumption. In *A Companion to Social Archaeology*, ed. L. Meskell and R. Preucel, 195–212. Oxford, U.K.: Blackwell Publishing.

Naranjo, Tessie. 1995. Thoughts on Migration by Santa Clara Pueblo. *Journal of Anthropological Archaeology* 14: 247–50.

Nash, Gary. 1991. *Creating the West: Historical Interpretations, 1890–1990*. Albuquerque: University of New Mexico Press.

Nassaney, Michael. 2002. Social Archaeology. In *The Foundations of Archaeology*, ed. D. Hardesty. Encyclopedia of Life Support Systems (EOLSS), developed under the auspices of the UNESCO. Oxford: Eolss Publishers (http://www.eolss.net).

———. 2004 Implementing Community Service Learning through Archaeological Practice. *Michigan Journal of Community Service Learning* 10 (3): 89–99.

Nassaney, Michael, and Marjorie Abel. 1993. The Political and Social Contexts of Cutlery Production in the Connecticut Valley. *Dialectical Anthropology* 18: 247–89.

———. 2000. Urban Spaces, Labor Organization, and Social Control: Lessons from New England's Nineteenth-Century Cutlery Industry. In *Lines That Divide: Historical Archaeologies of Race, Class, and Gender*, ed. J. Delle, S. Mrozowski, and R. Paynter, 239–75. Knoxville: University of Tennessee Press.

Newdick, Jane, and Lynn Rutherford. 1997. *The Tuscan Table*. London: Ebury Press.

New York Times. 2006. The Sago Mine Disaster (house editorial). January 5.

O'Neal, M. T. 1971. *Those Damn Foreigners*. Minerva, Calif.: Hollywood Press.

Orser, Charles. 1996. *A Historical Archaeology of the Modern World*. New York: Plenum Press.

———. 1998. The Archaeology of the African Diaspora. *Annual Review of Anthropology* 27: 63–82.

———. 2001. The Anthropology in American Historical Archaeology. *American Anthropologist* 103: 621–32.

———. 2003. The Archaeology of High Culture and Its Discontents. *Reviews in Anthropology* 32: 125–39.

Ortner, Sherry. 1991. Reading America: Preliminary Notes on Class and Culture. In *Recapturing Anthropology: Working in the Present*, ed. R. G. Fox, 163–89. Santa Fe, N.Mex.: School of American Research Press.

Otterbein, Keith. 2003. The Archaeology of War: An Alternative View. *Anthropology News*, December.

Palus, Matthew M., Mark P. Leone, and Matthew D. Cochran. 2006. Critical Archaeology: Politics Past and Present. In *Historical Archaeology*, ed. M. Hall and S. Silliman, 84–104. Oxford, U.K.: Blackwell Publishing.

Papanikolas, Zeese. 1982. *Buried Unsung: Louis Tikas and the Ludlow Massacre*. Salt Lake City: University of Utah Press.

———. 1995. *Trickster in the Land of Dreams*. Lincoln: University of Nebraska Press.

Patterson, Thomas. 1986. The Last Sixty Years: Toward a Social History of Americanist Archaeology in the United States. *American Anthropologist* 88: 7–26.

———. 1995. *Toward a Social History of Archaeology in the United States.* New York: Harcourt Brace.

Pauketat, Timothy. 2001. Practice and History in Archaeology. *Anthropological Theory* 1: 73–98.

Paynter, Robert. 1982. *Models of Spatial Inequality.* New York: Academic Press.

———. 1988. Steps to an Archaeology of Capitalism: Material Change and Class Analysis. In *The Recovery of Meaning: Historical Archaeology in the Eastern United States,* ed. M. Leone and P. Potter, 407–33. Washington, D.C.: Smithsonian Institution Press.

———. 1989. The Archaeology of Equality and Inequality. *Annual Review of Anthropology* 18: 369–99.

———. 2000a. Historical and Anthropological Archaeology: Forging Alliances. *Journal of Archaeological Research* 8: 1–37.

———. 2000b. Historical Archaeology and the Post-Columbian World of North America. *Journal of Archaeological Research* 8: 169–217.

Paynter, Robert, and Randall McGuire. 1991. The Archaeology of Inequality: Material Culture, Domination, and Resistance. In *The Archaeology of Inequality,* ed. R. McGuire and R. Paynter, 1–27. Oxford, U.K.: Basil Blackwell.

Pinsky, Valerie, and Alison Wylie, eds. 1989. *Critical Traditions in Contemporary Archaeology.* Cambridge: Cambridge University Press.

Pogliano, Felix. 1921. Letter to Mr. Luke Brennan, International Executive Board Member, District No. 15, U.M.W. of A. District 15 Correspondence. D15-1921, Nov.–Dec., United Mine Workers of America Archives, Pennsylvania State University, State College.

Poirier, David, and Robert Spude, eds. 1998. *America's Mining Heritage.* Washington, D.C.: National Park Service.

Pollack, Susan, and Reinhard Bernbeck. Forthcoming. "Grabe, wo Du stehst": An Archaeology of Perpetrators. In *Archaeology and Capitalism: From Ethics to Politics,* ed. P. Duke and Y. Hamilakis. London: University College London Press.

Potter, Parker B., Jr. 1992. Critical Archaeology: In the Ground and on the Street. *Historical Archaeology* 26: 117–29.

Praetzellis, Adrian, and Mary Praetzellis. 2001. Mangling Symbols of Gentility in the Wild West: Case Studies in Interpretive Archaeology. *American Anthropologist* 103: 645–54.

Preucel, Robert, ed. 1991. *Processual and Postprocessual Archaeologies: Multiple Ways of Knowing the Past.* Carbondale, Ill.: Center for Archaeological Investigations.

Preucel, Robert, and Ian Hodder. 1996. Communicating Present Pasts. In *Contemporary Archaeology in Theory,* ed. R. Preucel and I. Hodder, 3–20. Oxford, U.K.: Blackwell Publishing.

Prince, Gene. 1988. Photography for Discovery and Scale by Superimposing Old Photographs on the Present-Day Scene. *Antiquity* 62: 112–16.

Reed, John. 1955. The Colorado War. In *The Education of John Reed.* New York: International Publishers.

Roberts, Cecil. 2002. Protecting the Coal Miner. *Pittsburgh Gazette,* July 30.

———. 2006. Letter Opposing the Nomination of Richard Stickler as Assistant Secretary for Mine Safety and Health. United Mine Workers of America, March 8. Archived at www.umwa.org.

Rorty, Richard. 1989. *Contingency, Irony, and Solidarity.* Cambridge, Cambridge University Press.

———. 1991. *Objectivity, Relativism, and Truth.* Cambridge: Cambridge University Press.

———. 1998. *Achieving Our Country: Leftist Thought in Twentieth Century America.* Cambridge, Mass.: Harvard University Press.

———. 1999. *Philosophy and Social Hope.* New York: Penguin.

———. 2001. Justice as a Larger Loyalty. In *Richard Rorty: Critical Dialogues,* ed. M. Festenstein and S. Thompson, 223–37. Oxford, U.K.: Blackwell.

Roseberry, William. 1989. *Anthropologies and Histories.* New Brunswick, N.J.: Rutgers University Press.

Roth, Leland. 1992. Company Towns in the Western United States. In *The Company Town: Architecture and Society in the Early Industrial Age,* ed. J. Garner, 173–205. New York: Oxford University Press.

Rouse, Joseph. 2003. From Realism or Antirealism to Science as Solidarity. In *Richard Rorty,* ed. C. Guignon and D. Hiley, 81–104. Cambridge: Cambridge University Press.

Rowlands, Michael. 1982. Processual Archaeology as Historical Social Science. In *Theory and Explanation in Archaeology,* ed. C. Renfrew, M. Rowlands, and B. Segraves, 155–74. New York: Academic Press.

Sabloff, Jeremy, Lewis Binford, and Patricia McAnany. 1987. Understanding the Archaeological Record. *Antiquity* 61: 203–9.

Saitta, Dean J. 1983. The Poverty of Philosophy in Archaeology. In *Archaeological Hammers and Theories,* ed. J. Moore and A. Keene, 299–304. New York: Academic Press.

———. 1992. Radical Archaeology and Middle-Range Methodology. *Antiquity* 66: 886–97.

———. 2003. Ludlow Massacre. *Blue Sky Quarterly* (spring): 10. Pueblo, Colorado: Piñon Publishing.

———. 2004. Desecration at Ludlow. *New Labor Forum* 13: 86–89.

———. 2005. Dialoguing with the Ghost of Marx: Mode of Production in Archaeological Theory. *Critique of Anthropology* 25: 27–35.

———. 2006. Higher Education and the Dangerous Professor: Challenges for Anthropology. *Anthropology Today* 22 (4): 1–3.

Saitta, Dean J., Mark Walker, and Paul Reckner. 2005. Battlefields of Class Conflict: Ludlow Then and Now. *Journal of Conflict Archaeology* 1: 197–214.

Sampson, Joanne. 1999. *Remember Ludlow!* Denver: Colorado Historical Society, State Historical Fund.

Scamehorn, H. Lee. 1992. *Mill and Mine: The CF&I in the Twentieth Century.* Lincoln: University of Nebraska Press.

Schmidt, Peter, and Thomas Patterson, eds. 1995. *Making Alternative Histories: The Prac-*

tice of Archaeology and History in Non-Western Settings. Santa Fe, N.Mex.: School of American Research.

Schuldenrein, Joseph. 1999. Charting a Middle Ground in the NAGPRA Controversy: Secularism in Context. *Society for American Archaeology Newsletter* 22: 17.

Scott, Elizabeth, ed. 1994. *Those of Little Note: Gender, Race, and Class in Historical Archaeology.* Tucson: University of Arizona Press.

Scott, James. 1985. *Weapons of the Weak: Everyday Forms of Peasant Resistance.* New Haven, Conn.: Yale University Press.

Scott, Janny, and David Leonhardt. 2005. Class in America: Shadowy Lines That Still Divide. *New York Times,* May 15.

Scott, Shaunna. 1995. *Two Sides to Everything: The Cultural Construction of Class Consciousness in Harlan County, Kentucky.* Albany: State University of New York Press.

Seligman, Edwin R. 1914a. Colorado's Civil War and Its Lessons. *Leslie's Illustrated Weekly Newspaper,* November 5.

———. 1914b. The Crisis in Colorado. *Annalist,* May 4.

Shackel, Paul. 2000. Craft to Wage Labor: Agency and Resistance in American Historical Archaeology. In *Agency in Archaeology,* ed. M.-A. Dobres and J. Robb, 232–46. London: Routledge.

———. 2001. Public Memory and the Search for Power in American Historical Archaeology. *American Anthropologist* 103: 655–70.

———. 2004. Labor's Heritage: Remembering the American Industrial Landscape. *Historical Archaeology* 38: 44–58.

Shanks, Michael, and Randall McGuire. 1996. The Craft of Archaeology. *American Antiquity* 61: 75–88.

Shanks, Michael, and Christopher Tilley. 1987a. *Social Theory and Archaeology.* Albuquerque: University of New Mexico Press.

———. 1987b. *Re-constructing Archaeology: Theory and Practice.* Cambridge: Cambridge University Press.

Singleton, Teresa. 1995. The Archaeology of Slavery in North America. *Annual Review of Anthropology* 24: 119–40.

———. 2005. Before the Revolution: Archaeology and the African Diaspora on the Atlantic Seaboard. In *North American Archaeology,* ed. T. Pauketat and D. Loren, 319–36. Oxford, U.K.: Blackwell Publishing.

Singleton, Teresa, and Mark Bograd. 2000. Breaking Typological Barriers: Looking for the Colono in Colonoware. In *Lines That Divide: Historical Archaeologies of Race, Class, and Gender,* ed. J. Delle, S. Mrozowski, and R. Paynter, 3–21. Knoxville: University of Tennessee Press.

Smith, Henry. 1950. *Virgin Land: The American West as Symbol and Myth.* New York: Vintage Books.

Spector, Janet. 1993. *What This Awl Means: Feminist Archaeology at a Wahpeton Dakota Village.* Minneapolis: Minnesota Historical Society Press.

Spencer-Wood, Suzanne. 1991. Toward an Historical Archaeology of Materialistic Domestic Reform. In *The Archaeology of Inequality,* ed. R. McGuire and R. Paynter, 231–86. Oxford, U.K.: Basil Blackwell.

———. 1994. Diversity and Nineteenth-Century Domestic Reform: Relationships among Classes and Ethnic Groups. In *Those of Little Note: Gender, Race, and Class in Historical Archaeology,* ed. E. Scott, 175–208. Tucson: University of Arizona Press.

———. 2003. Gendering the Creation of Green Urban Landscapes in America at the Turn of the Century. In *Shared Spaces and Divided Places,* ed. D. Rotman and E. Savulis, 24–61. Knoxville: University of Tennessee Press.

Spriggs, Matthew, ed. 1984. *Marxist Perspectives in Archaeology.* Cambridge: Cambridge University Press.

Staub, Shalom. 1994. Cultural Conservation and Economic Recovery Planning: The Pennsylvania Heritage Parks Program. In *Conserving Culture: A New Discourse on Heritage,* ed. M. Hufford, 229–44. Urbana: University of Illinois Press.

Stegner, Wallace. 1982. Foreword. In *Buried Unsung: Louis Tikas and the Ludlow Massacre,* by Zeese Papanikolas, xiii–xix. Salt Lake City: University of Utah Press.

Stewart, Doug. 1997. Saving American Steel. *Smithsonian* (August): 86–93.

Strom, Shelly. 2000. OSM Haunted by the Past. *Business Journal of Portland,* November 6.

Sunsieri, Alvin. 1972. *The Ludlow Massacre: A Study in the Mis-employment of the National Guard.* Waterloo, Ia.: Salvadore Books.

Thomas, Julian. 2000. Reconfiguring the Social, Reconfiguring the Material. In *Social Theory in Archaeology,* ed. M. Schiffer, 143–55. Salt Lake City: University of Utah Press.

Tilley, Christopher. 1982. Social Formation, Social Structures, and Social Change. In *Symbolic and Structural Archaeology,* ed. I. Hodder, 26–38. Cambridge: Cambridge University Press.

———. 1989. Archaeology as Socio-Political Action in the Present. In *Critical Traditions in Contemporary Archaeology,* ed. V. Pinsky and A. Wylie, 104–16. Cambridge: Cambridge University Press.

Tomasky, Michael. 1997. Waltzing with Sweeny: Is the Academic Left Ready to Join the AFL-CIO? *Lingua Franca* (February): 40–47.

Trigger, Bruce. 1980. Archaeology and the Image of the American Indian. *American Antiquity* 45: 662–76.

———. 1981. Anglo-American Archaeology. *World Archaeology* 13: 138–55.

———. 1986. Prehistoric Archaeology and American Society. In *American Archaeology Past and Future,* ed. D. Meltzer, D. Fowler, and J. Sabloff, 187–215. Washington, D.C.: Smithsonian Institution Press.

———. 1989. *A History of Archaeological Thought.* Cambridge: Cambridge University Press.

Tringham, Ruth. 1991. Households with Faces: The Challenge of Gender in Prehistoric Architectural Remains. In *Engendering Archaeology,* ed. J. Gero and M. Conkey, 93–131. Oxford, U.K.: Basil Blackwell.

Trouillot, Michel-Ralph. 1995. *Silencing the Past: Power and the Production of History.* Boston: Beacon Press.

Tschauner, Hartmut. 1996. Middle-Range Theory, Behavioral Archaeology, and Post-empiricist Philosophy of Science in Archaeology. *Journal of Archaeological Method and Theory* 3: 1–30.

Turner, Frederick Jackson. 1920. *The Frontier in American History.* New York: Holt, Reinhart and Winston.

UMWA. 2006. UMWA President Roberts calls for "New Direction" from Bush Administration for MSHA Head. Press Release, October 2.

UMWJ. 1999. Lest We Forget: Ludlow Project Puts Massacre in Spotlight. *United Mine Workers Journal* (March–April): 12–13.

Urbina, Ian. 2006. Senators Have Strong Words for Mine Safety Officials. *New York Times,* January 24.

Urbina, Ian, and Gary Gately. 2006. Two Missing Workers Are Found Dead in West Virginia Mine. *New York Times,* January 22.

USCIR. 1916. *Industrial Relations: Final Report and Testimony Submitted to Congress by the Commission on Industrial Relations.* 64th Cong., 1st sess., S. Doc. 415.

U.S. Department of Labor. 2006. MINER Act Signed into Law. http://www.dol.gov/opa/media/press/msha/MSHA20061031.htm.

Vallejo, M. Edmund. 1998. Recollections of the Colorado Coal Strike, 1913–1914. In *La Gente: Hispano History and Life in Colorado,* ed. V. De Baca, 85–104. Denver: Colorado Historical Society.

Van Bueren, Thad, ed. 2002. Communities Defined by Work: Life in Western Work Camps. *Historical Archaeology* 36 (3).

Walker, Mark. 2000. Labor History at the Ground Level: Colorado Coalfield War Archaeological Project. *Labor's Heritage* 11: 58–75.

———. 2003. The Ludlow Massacre: Class, Warfare, and Historical Memory in Southern Colorado. *Historical Archaeology* 37: 66–80.

Walker, Mark, and Dean J. Saitta. 2002. Teaching the Craft of Archaeology: Theory, Practice, and the Field School. *International Journal of Historical Archaeology* 6: 199–207.

Walker, Ronald. 2005. Biased Reporting? *Archaeology* 58 (1): 9.

Wall, Diana de Zerega. 1991. Sacred Dinners and Secular Teas: Constructing Domesticity in Mid-19th-Century New York. *Historical Archaeology* 25 (4): 69–81.

———. 1994. *The Archaeology of Gender: Separating the Spheres in Urban America.* New York: Plenum.

———. 1999. Examining Gender, Class, and Ethnicity in Nineteenth-Century New York City. *Historical Archaeology* 33: 102–18.

Watkins, Joe. 1998. Native Americans, Western Science, and NAGPRA. *Society for American Archaeology Bulletin* 16 (5): 23.

Watson, Patty Jo. 1986. Archaeological Interpretation, 1985. In *American Archaeology Past and Future,* ed. D. Meltzer, D. Fowler, and J. Sabloff, 439–57. Washington, D.C.: Smithsonian Institution Press.

West, George P. 1915. *Report on the Colorado Strike.* Washington, D.C.: United States Commission on Industrial Relations.

White, Leslie. 1959. *The Evolution of Culture.* New York: McGraw Hill.

Whiteside, James. 1990. *Regulating Danger.* Lincoln: University of Nebraska Press.

Whitley, David. 1992. Prehistory and Post-positivist Science: A Prolegomenon to Cognitive Archaeology. In *Archaeological Method and Theory,* vol. 4, ed. M. Schiffer, 57–100. Tucson: University of Arizona Press.

Wilk, Richard. 1985. The Ancient Maya and the Political Present. *Journal of Anthropological Research* 41: 307–26.

Wilkie, Laurie. 2000. Culture Bought: Evidence of Creolization in the Consumer Goods of an Enslaved Bahamian Family. *Historical Archaeology* 34: 10–26.

———. 2003. *The Archaeology of Mothering: An African-American Midwife's Tale.* Oxford: Routledge.

———. 2005. Inessential Archaeologies: Problems of Exclusion in Americanist Archaeological Thought. *World Archaeology* 37: 337–51.

Wilkie, Laurie, and Kevin Bartoy. 2000. A Critical Archaeology Revisited. *Current Anthropology* 41: 747–78.

Williams, Raymond. 1989. *Resources of Hope: Culture, Democracy, Socialism.* London: Verso.

Wobst, H. Martin. 1977. Stylistic Behavior and Information Exchange. In *For the Director: Research Essays in Honor of James B. Griffin,* ed. C. Cleland, 317–42. Ann Arbor: University of Michigan, Museum of Anthropology.

———. 2000. Agency in (Spite of) Material Culture. In *Agency in Archaeology,* ed. M.-A. Dobres and J. Robb, 40–50. London: Routledge.

Wolf, Eric. 1982. *Europe and the People without History.* Berkeley: University of California Press.

———. 1990. Distinguished Lecture: Facing Power—Old Insights, New Questions. *American Anthropologist* 92: 586–96.

Wood, Margaret. 2001. Fighting for Our Homes: An Archaeology of Women's Domestic Labor and Social Change in a Working Class, Coal Mining Community, 1900–1930. Ph.D. dissertation, Syracuse University, Syracuse, N.Y.

———. 2002a. A House Divided: Changes in Women's Power within and outside the Household, 1900–1930. In *The Dynamics of Power,* ed. M. O'Donovan, 66–87. Carbondale, Ill.: Center for Archaeological Investigations.

———. 2002b. Moving toward Transformative Democratic Action through Archaeology. *International Journal of Historical Archaeology* 6: 187–98.

Wright, Erik Olin. 1993. Class Analysis, History, and Emancipation. *New Left Review* 202: 15–35.

Wurst, LouAnn. 1999. Internalizing Class in Historical Archaeology. *Historical Archaeology* 33: 7–21.

———. 2006. A Class All Its Own: Explorations of Class Formation and Conflict. In *Historical Archaeology,* ed. M. Hall and S. Silliman, 190–206. Oxford, U.K.: Blackwell Publishing.

Wurst, LouAnn, and Robert Fitts, eds. 1999. Confronting Class. *Historical Archaeology* 33 (1).

Wylie, Alison. 1989. Matters of Fact and Matters of Interest. In *Archaeological Approaches to Cultural Identity,* ed. S. Shennan, 94–109. London: Unwin Hyman.

———. 1993. Invented Lands/Discovered Pasts: The Westward Expansion of Myth and History. *Historical Archaeology* 27: 1–19.

———. 1995. Epistemic Disunity and Political Integrity. In *Making Alternative Histories: The Practice of Archaeology and History in Non-Western Settings,* ed. P. Schmidt and T. Patterson, 255–72. Santa Fe, N.Mex.: School of American Research.

Yamin, Rebecca. 2002. Children's Strikes, Parents' Rights: Paterson and Five Points. *International Journal of Historical Archaeology* 6: 113–26.

Yellen, Samuel. 1936. *American Labor Struggles.* New York: Harcourt, Brace.

Young, Amy. 2003. Gender and Landscape: A View from the Plantation Slave Community. In *Shared Spaces and Divided Places,* ed. D. Rotman and E. Savulis, 104–34. Knoxville: University of Tennessee Press.

Young, Amy, Michael Tuma, and Cliff Jenkins. 2001. The Role of Hunting to Cope with Risk at Saragossa Plantation, Natchez, Mississippi. *American Anthropologist* 103: 692–704.

Zimmerman, Larry. 1997. Remythologizing the Relationship between Indians and Archaeologists. In *Native Americans and Archaeologists,* ed. N. Swidler, K. Dongoske, R. Anyon, and A. Downer, pp. 44–56. Walnut Creek, Calif.: AltaMira Press.

———. 2001. Processing the Past: Interacting with Descendent Communities. Paper presented at the 2001 SAA meeting, New Orleans.

Zinn, Howard. 1970. *The Politics of History.* Boston: Beacon Press.

Index

Abel, Marjorie, 40–41

Adaptation, 19, 21, 22, 27

Africa, 29–30, 35, 36, 37

African-Americans: and children's toys, 81; collective ethos among, 85; and dining etiquette, 80; foods purchased by, 76; and landscapes, 39–40; and material culture, 35, 36, 37; occupations of, 49, 81, 84; as slaves, 36, 85

African diaspora, 35

Agency. *See* Individual agency

Aguilar, Colo., 55

Alabama, 94, 96

Ammons, Elias, 56, 59, 60, 69

"Ancient Maya and the Political Present, The" (Wilk), 1

Animals: cattle, 78; chickens, 84; deer, 40; goats, 78; pigs, 78; rabbits, 40, 78, 84; raccoons, 40; sheep, 78–79; squirrels, 40; toads, spadefoot, 78

Annapolis, Md., 30, 37, 42, 43, 76

Anthropology, 26, 27, 32, 109, 110

Aracoma Coal Company, 95

Archaeological techniques: "dog leash" collections, 69; excavation, 7, 13, 36, 38, 41, 42, 65–66, 67, 72, 73, 74, 75, 76, 78, 79, 81, 82, 83, 84, 87, 96; excavation, block, 73; faunal analysis, 78; mechanical scrapes, 60; photo-overlay investigation, 68–69; settlement catchment analysis, 20; surface observations, 65–66; surveys, 65; surveys, ground-penetrating radar, 66, 89; surveys, metal-detector, 66, 89; testing, auger, 87; testing, shovel, 65

Archaeology: anthropologists and, 27; audiences for, 1–2, 4, 7, 10–11, 12, 14, 15, 21–22, 108, 111, 112; and change, 111; and class, 106, 109, 110; of collective action, 108–9; comparative, 110; and contemporary life, 4–5, 108; contextual, 21–24; critical, 3–4, 5, 9, 91, 92, 103, 109; critiques of, 7, 10; and culture, 18–25; and descendant communities, 2, 10–11, 32; development of, 18; emancipatory, 3, 4, 6, 7, 8, 9, 10, 25, 31, 43, 90, 106, 110, 111; evolutionary, 10; explanatory, 3, 7, 9, 10, 20, 28, 43, 90; focuses of, 12–13; future of, 109; and globalization, 2; historical, 4, 5–6, 7, 30, 37, 110, 111–12; identity-oriented, 43; inclusiveness of, 15, 101; and inequality, 106, 108–9; influences on, 19; interpretative, 10, 21; and middle class, 108, 111, 112; and objectivity, 11–12; and politics, 1, 2–3, 9; postprocessual, 21–24, 31–32, 111–12; and pragmatism, 9–17, 32; prehistoric, 111–12; as process, 16–17; processual, 19–20, 21–22, 23, 27, 28, 30, 31, 111–12; processual-plus, 24; and public good, 107; scientific nature of, 1, 2–3, 10–11, 15, 18, 19, 106; social, 8–9, 92; and social change, 3; social context of, 1–3; social relevance of, 103; and women, 12, 37; and working class, 12–13, 106

Archaeology, 1, 105

"Archaeology as Anthropology" (Binford), 27–28

Architecture: and class, 30, 39, 42, 43; company housing, 85; and domestic reform, 38; foundations for, 84, 85; Lowcountry, 37; materials for, 51, 84, 85; miners and, 51; slaves and, 35, 39

Army, U.S., 59

Dean J. Saitta is a professor of anthropology at the University of Denver.
His research interests are in North American archaeology, prehistory of the
American Southwest, American labor history, comparative architectural and
urban form, and memory and monumentality. He is coauthor of *Denver: An
Archaeological History* (2001).